1499

The Emotion Thesaurus:

A Writer's Guide To Character Expression

Angela Ackerman
& Becca Puglisi

First print edition, May 2012
ISBN-13: 978-1475004953
ISBN-10: 1475004958

Edited in part by: Sharon Knauer

Book cover design by: Scarlett Rugers Design 2012
scarlettrugers.com

book formatting by: CyberWitch Press
cyberwitchpress.com

ABOUT THE AUTHORS

Angela Ackerman is a member of the SCBWI and writes on the darker side of Middle Grade and Young Adult. She believes in the monster under the bed, eats French fries and ice cream together and is dedicated to paying it forward however she can. Angela lives in Calgary, Alberta in the shadow of the Canadian Rockies with her husband, two children, dog and zombie-like fish.

Becca Puglisi is a YA fantasy and historical fiction writer, magazine author, and member of the SCBWI. She resides in sunny south Florida, where she likes to watch movies, drink caffeinated beverages, and eat foods that aren't good for her. She lives with her husband and two children.

Together, Angela and Becca host Writers Helping Writers (formerly *The Bookshelf Muse*), an award-winning online resource that offers a number of different thesauri to aid authors in their descriptive writing efforts. You can visit them online at http://writershelpingwriters.net.

MORE WRITERS HELPING WRITERS BOOKS

The Positive Trait Thesaurus: A Writer's Guide to Character Attributes

The Negative Trait Thesaurus: A Writer's Guide to Character Flaws

ACKNOWLEDGEMENTS

First and foremost, we want to thank readers of *The Bookshelf Muse* and *Writers Helping Writers* for their support, encouragement, and kind words. You made us see the need for a book version of *The Emotion Thesaurus*, and your belief in us made it happen.

We also want to acknowledge the very important members of our first critique group: Helen (Bookish), Roy (Grampy), Madeline (Maddog), Joan (Unohoo), and Laura (Goofus). These Critique Circle writers helped us kick start this list and our respective writing careers. Our deepest appreciation also goes to our friend and editor Sharon, who encouraged us when we needed it most.

We also owe a huge debt to the writing community at large. The writers we have met online, at conferences, at face-to-face groups, and in our own communities have been so generous with their knowledge and optimism, enabling us each to grow as writers. We love being part of this group.

And finally, the biggest shout out goes to our families, who supported us though they couldn't see the vision, encouraged us when we struggled, and provided the business savvy we were lacking. We owe it all to you.

~To AAD and SDJ, with all our love~

TABLE OF CONTENTS

INTRODUCTION

THE POWER OF EMOTION

All successful novels, no matter what genre, have one thing in common: emotion. It lies at the core of every character's decision, action, and word, all of which drive the story. Without emotion, a character's personal journey is pointless. Stakes cease to exist. The plot line becomes a dry riverbed of meaningless events that no reader will take time to read. Why? Because above all else, readers pick up a book to have an emotional experience. They read to connect with characters who provide entertainment and whose trials may add meaning to their own life journeys.

As emotional beings, feelings propel us. They drive our choices, determine who we spend time with, and dictate our values. Emotion also fuels our communication, allowing us to share meaningful information and beliefs with others. And while it may seem that most exchanges happen through conversation, studies show that 93% of all communication is nonverbal. Even in instances where we try not to show our feelings, we are still sending messages through body language. Because of this, each of us becomes adept at reading others without a word being said.

As writers, we must take our innate skills of observation and transfer them to the page. Readers have high expectations. They don't want to be told how a character feels; they want to experience the emotion for themselves. To make this happen, we must ensure that our characters express their emotions in ways that are both recognizable and compelling to read.

VERBAL AND NONVERBAL COMMUNICATION

Dialogue is a proven vehicle for expressing a character's thoughts, beliefs, and opinions, but it cannot deliver a full emotional experience by itself. To convey feelings well, a writer must also utilize nonverbal communication, which can be broken down into three elements: physical signals (body language and actions), internal sensations (visceral reactions) and mental responses (thoughts).

PHYSICAL SIGNALS are how our bodies outwardly respond when we experience emotion. The stronger the feeling, the more the body reacts and the less conscious control we have over movement. Because characters are unique, they will express themselves in a specific way. Combine the vast number of physical signals with the individuality of each character, and a writer's options for showing emotion through body language and action are virtually limitless.

MENTAL RESPONSES act as a window into the thought process that corresponds with an emotional experience. Thoughts are not always rational and can skip from topic to topic with incredible speed. Utilizing thought as a way to express emotion is an excellent way to convey to the reader how a character sees their world. Thoughts add a layer of meaning by illustrating how people, places, and events affect the POV (point of view) character and can also be an excellent way to demonstrate voice.

INTERNAL SENSATIONS are the most powerful form of nonverbal communication and should be used with the most caution. These visceral reactions (breathing, heart rate, light-headedness, adrenaline spikes, etc.) are raw and uncontrolled, triggering the fight-or-flight response. Because these are instinctive body responses, all people experience them. As such, readers will recognize and connect with them on a primal level.

The very nature of these heightened visceral reactions requires writers to take special care when using them. Relying too much on internal sensations can create melodrama. Also, because visceral reactions are limited, a writer can inadvertently use clichéd phrasings when describing them. A light touch is needed with this type of nonverbal communication, as a little goes a long way.

THE BALANCING ACT

It is easy to see the power of emotion and how it connects a reader to the story and characters. The difficulty comes in writing it well. Each scene must achieve a balance between showing too little feeling and showing too much. Above all, the emotional description needs to be fresh and engaging. This is a tall order for writers who tend to reuse the same emotional indicators over and over.

The Emotion Thesaurus addresses this difficulty by helping writers brainstorm new ideas for expressing a character's emotional state. But what about other pitfalls associated with portraying emotion? The following section explores a few of these common trouble spots and suggests techniques for overcoming them.

WRITING NONVERBAL EMOTION: AVOIDING COMMON PROBLEMS

TELLING

By definition, nonverbal emotion can't be told. It has to be shown. This makes it difficult to write because telling is easier than showing. Here's an example:

> Mr. Paxton's eyes were sad as he gave her the news. "I'm sorry, JoAnne, but your position with the company is no longer necessary."
> Instantly, JoAnne was angrier than she'd ever been in her life.

This exchange is fairly easy to write—but not so easy to read. Readers are smart and can figure things out for themselves. They don't want to have the scene explained to them, which is what happens when a writer tells how a character feels. Another problem with telling is that it creates distance between the reader and your characters, which is rarely a good idea. In the preceding example, the reader sees that Mr. Paxton is reluctant to give JoAnne the bad news and that JoAnne is angry about it. But you don't want the reader to only see what's happening; you want them to feel the emotion, and to experience it along with the character. To accomplish this, writers need to show the character's physical and internal responses rather than stating the emotion outright.

> JoAnne sat on the chair's edge, spine straight as a new pencil, and stared into Mr. Paxton's face. Sixteen years she'd given him—days she was sick, days the kids were sick—making the trip back and forth across town on that sweaty bus. Now he wouldn't even look at her, just kept fiddling with her folder and rearranging the fancy knickknacks on his desk. Clearly, he didn't want to give her the news, but she wasn't about to make it easy for him.
> The vinyl of her purse crackled and she lightened her grip on it. Her picture of the kids was in there and she didn't want it creased.
> Mr. Paxton cleared his throat for the hundredth time. "JoAnne...Mrs. Benson...it appears that your position with the company is no longer—"
> JoAnne jerked to her feet, sending her chair flying over the tile. It hit the wall with a satisfying bang as she stormed from the office.

This scene gives the reader a much better opportunity to share in JoAnne's anger. Through the use of sensory details, a well chosen simile, specific verbs, and body cues that correspond with the featured emotion, readers can see that JoAnne is angry, but they also feel it—in the straightness of her spine and the cheap vinyl in her grip, in the force it takes to send a chair flying across the room simply from the act of standing.

An example like this also reveals a lot about the character. JoAnne is not well-to-do. She has children to support. She may be angry, but she's also strong minded, family oriented, and proud. This information rounds out JoAnne's character and makes her more relatable to the reader.

Showing takes more work then telling, as word count alone will indicate, but it pays off by drawing the reader closer to the character and helping to create empathy. Once in a great while, it's acceptable to tell the reader what the character is feeling: when you have to pass on information quickly, or when you need a crisp sentence to convey a shift in mood or attention. But the other ninety-nine times out of a hundred, put in the extra work and you will reap the benefits of showing.

CLICHÉD EMOTIONS

- The grin that stretches from ear to ear
- A single tear pooling in the eye before coursing down the cheek
- Quivering knees that knock together

Clichés in literature are vilified for good reason. They're a sign of lazy writing, a result of settling on the easy phrase because coming up with something new is too hard. Writers often fall back on clichés because, technically, these tired examples work. That grin implies happiness as certainly as knee knocking indicates fear. Unfortunately, phrases like these lack depth because they don't allow for a range of emotions. That single tear tells you that the person is sad, but how upset is she? Sad enough to sob? Shriek? Collapse? Will she even be crying five minutes from now? To relate to your character, the reader needs to know the depth of emotion being experienced.

When writing a certain emotion, think about your body and what happens to it when you're feeling that way. Excitement, for example. The heart races and the pulse quickens. Legs bounce. The speech of a methodical person becomes fast paced with streaming words. The voice is pitched higher and louder. For any given emotion, there are literally dozens of internal and external changes that, when referenced, will show the reader what your character is feeling. The lists in this thesaurus are great for providing ideas, but your own observations are just as helpful. Watch people—real flesh-and-blood specimens at the mall or characters in movies. Note how they act when they're confused or overwhelmed or irritable. The face is the easiest to notice but the rest of the body is just as telling. Don't overlook changes in a person's voice, speech, or overall bearing and posture.

Secondly, know your character. Individuals do things differently—even mundane activities like brushing their teeth, driving, or making dinner. Emotions are no exception. Not every character will shout and throw things when angry. Some speak in quiet voices. Others go completely silent. Many, for various reasons, will cover their anger and act like they're not upset at all. Whatever your character is feeling, describe the emotion in a way that is specific to him or her, and you're almost guaranteed to write something new and evocative.

MELODRAMA

If all emotions were of average intensity, they'd be easier to describe. But emotions vary in strength. Take fear, for instance. Depending upon the severity of the situation, a person might feel anything from unease to anxiety to paranoia or terror. Extreme emotions will require extreme descriptors, while others are relatively subtle and must be described as such. Unfortunately, many writers make the mistake of assuming that to be gripping, emotion must be dramatic. Sad people should burst into tears. Joyful characters must express their glee by jumping up and down. This kind of writing results in melodrama, which leads to a sense of disbelief in the reader because, in real life, emotion isn't always so demonstrative.

To avoid melodrama, recognize that emotions run along a continuum, from mild to extreme. For each situation, know where your character is along that continuum and choose appropriate descriptors. Just as extreme emotions call for extreme indicators, temperate emotions should be expressed subtly. The indicators for intermediate emotions will lie somewhere in the middle.

It's also very important that your character follows a smooth emotional arc. Consider the following example:

> Mack tapped his thumb against the steering wheel, one arm dangling out the window. He smiled at Dana but she just sat there, twisting that one loop of hair around her finger.
>
> "Worried about your interview tomorrow?" he asked.
>
> "A little. It's a great opportunity but the timing's awful. There's too much going on." She sighed. "I've been thinking about cutting back. Simplifying."
>
> "Good idea." He nodded along with the radio and waved at the biker who thundered past on his Harley.
>
> "I'm glad you agree." She faced him. "I think we should break up."
>
> His foot slipped off the gas pedal. The air grew heavy, making it hard to breathe. The car veered toward the middle line and he let it drift, not caring whether he lived or died.

Unless Mack has a psychological reason for doing so, he shouldn't jump from placidity to depression in a matter of seconds. A realistic progression would be to move from contentment to shock, then disbelief, and finally to grief. Done thoughtfully, this emotional arc can be shown with relatively few words:

> "I'm glad you agree." She faced him. "I think we should break up."
>
> His foot slipped off the gas pedal. "Break up? What are you talking about?"
>
> "Mack. We've been headed this way for awhile, you know that."
>
> He gripped the steering wheel and took deep breaths. Sure, things had been rough lately, and she kept talking about needing some time to herself, but she always came around. And she'd definitely never uttered the words, "break up."
>
> "Look, Dana—"
>
> "Please, don't. You can't talk me out of it this time." She stared at the dashboard. "I'm sorry."
>
> His insides twisted. He darted a look at Dana, but she was curled against the window now, both hands resting easy in her lap.
>
> He gaped at her. They were totally breaking up.

Make sure that your character's feelings progress realistically. Map out the emotional journey within the scene to avoid unintended melodrama.

All of this is not to say that real life doesn't produce extreme emotion. Birth, death, loss, change—some situations call for intense responses that may go on for awhile. Many writers, in an admirable attempt to maintain believability, try to recreate these events in real time. This results in long paragraphs or even pages of high emotion and, inevitably, melodrama. Though real life can sustain this kind of intensity for long periods of time, it's nearly impossible for the written word to do so in a way that readers will accept.

In these situations, avoid melodrama by abbreviating. This method is often used for other real-life scenarios—conversations, for instance. Small talk is left out to keep the pace moving forward. Mundane tasks are also cut short, because the reader doesn't need (or want) to see the entire car washed, a piece at a time, while Bob ponders a problem at work. In the same way, extensive emotional scenes should be long enough to convey the appropriate information, but not so long that you lose the audience. Write the emotion well, develop empathy in your reader, maximize the words that you do use, but don't overstay your welcome.

OVER-RELIANCE ON DIALOGUE OR THOUGHTS

Because nonverbal writing is so hard to master, it makes sense that some writers shy away from it, choosing to rely more on thoughts or dialogue to express what a character is feeling. But an over-reliance on either leads to problems.

"Are—Are you sure?" I asked.

"Without a doubt," Professor Baker replied. "It was neck-and-neck right up to the end, but you came out ahead. Congratulations, William!"

"I can't believe it," I said. "Valedictorian! I'm so happy!"

Word choice is important in expressing emotion, but it will only go so far. After that, the writer is reduced to weak techniques like telling the reader what's being felt (I'm so happy) and over-using exclamation points to show intensity. Without any action to break up the dialogue, the conversation also sounds stilted.

On the other hand, conveying emotion solely through thoughts has its problems, too.

My pulse was pounding somewhere in the 160 range. I did it! Valedictorian! I was sure Nathan would come out ahead—he was a phenom in the physics lab, and he'd been a ghost at school all month, practically living in the library.

I threw my arms around Professor Baker. I'd think about this later and cringe with embarrassment, but right now, I didn't care. I'd done it! Take THAT, Nathan Shusterman!

Technically, there's nothing wrong with this sample. Bodily cues, both internal and external, are included. It's clear to the reader that William is excited. Yet it doesn't ring true. Why? Because this monologue screams for verbal interaction with others. Professor Baker is there and has clearly been talking to William. For William to be so incredibly excited and not say anything comes across as...odd.

Internal dialogue is an important part of any story. There are many scenes and scenarios where a paragraph or more of contemplation is appropriate. This isn't one of them. For this scene, and for the majority of scenes, emotion is much more effectively conveyed through a mixture of dialogue, thoughts, and body language.

My pulse jittered somewhere around the 160 mark. No, I'd heard him wrong, been tricked by an over-active, sleep-deprived, twisted imagination.

"Are—" I cleared my throat. "Are you sure?"

"It was neck-and-neck right up to the end, but you came out ahead. Congratulations, William."

The leather chair squeaked as I collapsed into it. Valedictorian. How'd I beat out Nathan, who'd been a ghost all month, practically living in the library? Not to mention that B- I scraped in physics.

"But I did it," I whispered.

The professor stood to shake my hand. I jumped up and threw my arms around him, lifting him off the floor. Later, I'd remember this and die of embarrassment, but right now I didn't care.

"I did it! Take THAT, Nathan Shusterman!"

"Knew you had it in you," the professor said in a strangled voice.

When expressing emotion, vary your vehicles, using both verbal and nonverbal techniques for maximum impact.

MISUSING BACKSTORY TO ENHANCE READER EMPATHY

Every character is unique, influenced largely by events from the past. One surefire way to gain reader empathy is to reveal why a character is the way he is. Take the movie *Jaws*, for example. The first glimpse we have of shark hunter Quint, he's raking his none-too-clean fingernails down a chalkboard. Hardly endearing. As the movie progresses, the viewer's dislike is justified through his crass manners and bullying of young Mr. Hooper. But once he tells his story of the sinking of the *Indianapolis* and his five days and nights treading water with the sharks, the viewer understands how he became so hardened. His behavior hasn't changed and we still don't like him very much, but we empathize with him now. We wish him better than what life has served up to him.

This is just one example of the importance of backstory in building reader empathy. People are products of their past. As the author, it's important for you to know why your characters are the way they are and to pass that information along to readers. For more help on developing your character's backstory and discovering his resulting personality, we recommend *The Positive Trait Thesaurus: A Writer's Guide to Character Attributes* and *The Negative Trait Thesaurus: A Writer's Guide to Character Flaws*.

The difficulty comes in knowing how much of the past to share. Many writers, in an attempt to gain reader empathy, reveal too much. Excessive backstory slows the pace and can bore readers, tempting them to skip ahead to the good stuff. Undoubtedly, Quint's path to crusty and crazy contained more than that one unfortunate event, but the rest didn't need to be shared. That one story, artfully told, was enough.

In order to avoid using too much backstory, determine which details from your character's past are necessary to share. Dole them out through the context of the present-time story to keep the pace moving. For inspiration, consider your favorite literary characters, even those who may have been unlikable. Revisit their stories to see what clues from the past the author chose to reveal, and how it was done.

Backstory is tricky to write well. As is true of so many areas of writing, balance is the key.

USING THE EMOTION THESAURUS

We've established that emotion powers a scene, and when written well, propels readers out of apathy and into the character's emotional experience. Writing authentic emotion is not always easy, but to create breakout fiction, writers must come up with fresh ideas to express their characters' feelings.

Emotion is strongest when both verbal and nonverbal communication are used in tandem. The Emotion Thesaurus can supply that critical nonverbal element writers need to fire up an emotional hit that will leave a lasting impression on readers. Here are some final ideas on how to use this thesaurus to its fullest:

IDENTIFY THE ROOT EMOTION

Certain situations can arouse a single, easily identifiable emotion. But more often than not, human beings feel more than one thing at a time. If you are struggling with how to convey this conflict to the reader, take a step back and identify your character's root emotion. This is the catalyst that dictates any other feelings your character might also experience. Once you've found the root emotion, look to the corresponding thesaurus entry for a range of suggestions. The MAY ESCALATE TO field can also provide a logical progression for where your character's feelings might be headed. Once you've clearly shown the root emotion, you can layer other emotions on to a lesser degree and map out the full experience.

UTILIZE THE SETTING

Characters don't live in bubbles—they interact with the world around them. This is especially true when emotions come into play. A character in the kitchen might sweep a wine glass off the counter in a fit of rage, but in an office setting, the same anger may require some control, ranging from a slammed office door to tense posture and fingers pounding the keyboard. When referring to the thesaurus entries, a writer should keep in mind the character's setting in order to create organic and unique emotional responses.

LESS IS MORE

Using too many cues to describe a character's feelings can slow the pace and dilute the reader's emotional experience. Sometimes this happens when a writer fails to identify and focus first on the root emotion. Other times, it's the result of choosing too many weak descriptors. Strong imagery will paint an immediate picture, so always strive to create concrete body language for the reader to interpret. Watch for overlong emotional passages that slow the action. Always think like a reader, and keep those pages turning.

TWIST THE CLICHÉ

Whenever possible, writers should use fresh ideas to convey emotion. But let's face it...some descriptors work well. That's why they crop up in novels again and again. Each thesaurus entry includes a myriad of possible cues; if you find yourself leaning toward a traditional response like eye rolling or fist clenching that can be seen as cliché, twist it first.

Take shivering, for example—a common visceral indicator to imply fear or discomfort. Shivers run up the spine, down the spine...these are tired phrases that can turn off readers. Sure, the sensation fits, but why not come up with something new? Why couldn't a shiver swarm over the back of the legs? How about using a simile that likens a shiver to leaf-cutter ants marching along a vine? Better yet, don't call it a shiver at all. Instead, describe the sensations of tightening skin or hair being raised. Never be afraid to experiment. There are many ways to take a tired expression and twist it into something unique.

VIEW ENTRIES AS A LAUNCHING POINT

Body movement, actions, visceral sensations, and thoughts are as individual as the characters experiencing them. The list accompanying each thesaurus entry is not designed as a one-size-fits-all set of options. It is meant, rather, to prompt writers to think beyond the basics. Each character comes from a different background and has a unique personality. Their comfort level around others will also influence how they express emotion. With this in mind, entries should serve as a brainstorming tool and encourage writers to take the next step and create fresh, individual ways to show a character's emotional state.

TRY RELATED EMOTIONS

If you're struggling to find the perfect physical response, visceral reaction, or thought, try reading through the entries of similar emotions. Each entry contains different cues. Studying the lists for related feelings may spark an idea for something new.

VISCERAL REACTIONS AS PHYSICAL INDICATORS

Sometimes, the strongest emotional responses are instinctive (visceral) ones that occur mostly internally and are therefore difficult for others to notice. This becomes a problem for writers who want to show a character's emotion while remaining true to their third- or first-person point of view. In these cases, writers should focus on visceral reactions that have a physical "tell" attached to them. For example, sweating, blushing and shakiness have an external component that can be seen by others. Utilizing these cues allows a writer to describe a visceral reaction without damaging the integrity of the point of view. Because of the external signs that accompany these unique internal sensations, we have included them under the PHYSICAL SIGNALS heading.

A FINAL WORD

Our hope for this book is that it will help writers brainstorm unique ways to express character emotion. These entries are only a starting point, but we hope *The Emotion Thesaurus* will become a useful companion on your writing journey, and will travel with you from book to book. Happy writing!

THE EMOTION THESAURUS

ADORATION

DEFINITION: the act of worship; to view as divine
NOTE: *the subject of adoration can be a person or thing*

PHYSICAL SIGNALS:
Lips parting
A slack or soft expression
Walking quickly to erase the distance
Mimicking body language (of the subject)
Touching one's mouth or face
Reaching out to brush, touch or grasp
Steady eye contact, large pupils
Leaning forward
Stroking one's own neck or arm as a surrogate
Pointing one's torso and feet toward the subject
A flushed appearance
Nodding while the subject speaks
Smiling
Open body posture
Releasing an appreciative sigh
Laying a hand over the heart
Frequently moistening the lips
Pressing palms lightly against the cheeks
Skimming fingertips along the jaw line
Eyes that are bright, glossy
Agreement (murmuring affirmations)
Speaking praise and compliments
Keeping trinkets, pictures, or articles of the subject
Constantly talking about the subject to others
Rapt attention, still posture
Becoming unaware of one's environment or other people
A radiant glow
Visible shakiness
Reduced blinking
Closing the eyes to savor the experience
Speaking with a soft voice or tone
A voice that cracks with emotion

INTERNAL SENSATIONS:
Quickening heartbeat
Breathlessness
Feeling one's pulse in the throat
Mouth drying
Throat growing thick

Rising body temperature
Tingling nerve endings

MENTAL RESPONSES:
A desire to move closer or touch
Fixating one's thoughts on the subject
Acute listening and observation
Ignoring distractions
An inability to see the subject's flaws or faults

CUES OF ACUTE OR LONG-TERM ADORATION:
Obsession
Fantasizing
Believing that the feelings are mutual
A sense of destiny (of belonging together)
Stalking
Writing and sending letters, email, and gifts
Taking risks or breaking laws to be near or with the subject
Weight loss
Poor sleep patterns
Jealousy towards those interacting with the subject
Taking on traits or mannerisms of the subject
Carrying something that represents the subject (a picture, clothes)
Possessiveness
MAY ESCALATE TO: LOVE (106), DESIRE (50), FRUSTRATION (78), HURT (92)

CUES OF SUPPRESSED ADORATION:
Clenching or hiding one's hands to hide sweating or shaking
Avoiding conversations about the subject
Watching or observing from afar
Staying out of the subject's proximity
Blushing
Sneaking looks at the subject
Creating chance run ins
Writing secret letters, keeping a diary
Lying about one's feelings regarding the subject

WRITER'S TIP: *Body cues should create a strong mental picture. If the movement is too drawn out or complicated, the emotional meaning behind the gesture may be lost.*

AGITATION

DEFINITION: feeling upset or disturbed; a state of unrest

PHYSICAL SIGNALS:
A reddening of the face
A sheen of sweat on the cheeks, chin, and forehead
Hands moving in jerks
Rubbing the back of the neck
Patting pockets or digging in a purse, looking for something lost
Clumsiness due to rushing (knocking things over, bumping tables)
A gaze that bounces from place to place
An inability to stay still
Jamming or cramming things away without care
Abrupt movement (causing a chair to tip or scuff the floor loudly)
Flapping hands
Becoming accident prone (bashing one's hip on a desk corner, etc.)
Dragging the hands through the hair repeatedly
Forgetting words, being unable to articulate thoughts
Backtracking to try and undo something said in haste
Adjusting one's clothing
Avoiding eye contact
A wavering voice
Not knowing where to look or go
Guarding one's personal space
Taking too long to answer a question or respond
Throat clearing
Overusing *ums, ahs,* and other verbal hesitations
Turning away from others
A bobbing Adam's apple
Pacing
Making odd noises in the throat
Rapid lip movement as one tries to find the right thing to say
Flinching if touched
Minimizing another's compliments
Fanning self
Unbuttoning a top shirt button
Tugging at a tie, collar, or scarf

INTERNAL SENSATIONS:
Excessive saliva
Feeling overheated
Stiffening hair on the nape of the neck
Light-headedness
Short, fast breaths

Sweating
Tingling skin as sweat forms

MENTAL RESPONSES:
Mounting frustration that causes thoughts to blank
Compounding mistakes
A tendency to lie to cover up or excuse
Anger at oneself for freezing up
Trying to pinpoint the source of discomfort
Mentally ordering oneself to calm down, relax

CUES OF ACUTE OR LONG-TERM AGITATION:
Flight response (looking for an escape or fleeing the room)
Snapping at others, or adopting a defensive tone
Scattering papers and files in a frantic search
MAY ESCALATE TO: ANNOYANCE (26), FRUSTRATION (78),
ANXIETY (30), ANGER (22)

CUES OF SUPPRESSED AGITATION:
Changing the subject
Making excuses
Joking to lighten the mood
Staying busy with tasks to avoid dealing with the source of the emotion
Shifting attention to others, putting them in the spotlight

WRITER'S TIP: A ticking clock can ramp up the emotions in any scene. As the character hurries to complete a task or meet a need, mistakes caused by rushing open the door for a richer emotional ride.

AMAZEMENT

DEFINITION: overwhelming astonishment or wonder

PHYSICAL SIGNALS:
Widening of the eyes
A slack mouth
Becoming suddenly still
Sucking in a quick breath
A hand covering one's mouth
Stiffening posture
Giving a small yelp
Rapid blinking followed by open staring
Flinching or starting, the body jumping slightly
Taking a step back
A slow, disbelieving shake of the head
Voicing wonder: *I can't believe it!* or *Look at that!*
Pulling out a cell phone to record the event
Glancing to see if others are experiencing the same thing
Pressing a hand against one's chest, fingers splayed out
Leaning in
Moving closer
Reaching out or touching
Eyebrows raising
Lips parting
A wide smile
Spontaneous laughter
Pressing palms to cheeks
Fanning oneself
Repeating the same things over and over
Squealing dramatically

INTERNAL SENSATIONS:
A heart that seems to freeze, then pound
Rushing blood
Rising body temperature
Tingling skin
Stalled breaths
Adrenaline spikes

MENTAL RESPONSES:
Momentarily forgetting all else
Wanting to share the experience with others
Giddiness
Disorientation

Euphoria
An inability to find words

CUES OF ACUTE OR LONG-TERM AMAZEMENT:
A racing heartbeat
Shortness of breath
Knees going weak
Feeling overwhelmed, as if the room is closing in
Collapsing
MAY ESCALATE TO: CURIOSITY (40), DISBELIEF (58), EXCITEMENT (74)

CUES OF SUPPRESSED AMAZEMENT:
Holding oneself tight (self-hugging)
Walking in jerky, self-contained strides
Clamping the hands to the chest
Looking down or away to hide one's expression
Eyes widening a bit before control is asserted
Mouth snapping shut
A stony expression
Taking a seat to hide the emotion
Making excuses if reaction is noticed
Stuttering, stammering

WRITER'S TIP: *To add another layer to an emotional experience, look for symbolism within the character's current setting. What unique object within the location can the character make note of that perfectly embodies the emotion they are feeling inside?*

AMUSEMENT

DEFINITION: appealing to the sense of humor; to feel entertainment or delight

PHYSICAL SIGNALS:
A shiny or rosy face
Raised or wiggling eyebrows
Snorting, laughing
Chuckling or cackling
Displaying a wide grin
Exchanging knowing looks with others
Witty commentary
Making joking observations
Turning away and bursting out in laughter
A playful pinch, nudge, or shove
Eyes squinting, lit with an inner glow or twinkle of mischief
Smirking or offering a bemused smile
Clutching at another person for support
Gasping for air
Slapping one's knees or thighs
Drumming feet against the floor
Falling against someone, shoulder to shoulder
"Drunken" behavior (weaving, staggering)
Repeating the punch line or a select word to spur more laughter
A high voice
Holding one's sides
Whimpers of mirth
Spewing food or drink if laughter hits while eating or drinking
Falling to the ground, rolling on the floor
Nose running, sniffing
Crashing into things, being clumsy but not caring
A wide-eyed look that gets others dissolving into laughter again
A belly laugh
Holding onto a chair or wall for support
Giggling, making faces, winking
Plucking at clothes to cool down

INTERNAL SENSATIONS:
Pain in the ribs or stomach
Wheezy breath
Body temperature jumping up
Weakness in limbs, especially the knees

MENTAL RESPONSES:
A need to sit down

20

Replaying the humorous event
Embellishing the event in one's mind, increasing the mirth
Wanting to keep the amusement going by adding to it with others

CUES OF ACUTE OR LONG-TERM AMUSEMENT:
Uncontrollable laughter
Laughing so hard it becomes soundless
Body quaking
Shaking the head emphatically
A loss of body control (weak muscles, having a hard time staying upright)
Begging people to stop
An inability to form words
Breathlessness
Eyes tearing
A sweaty, disheveled appearance
Loss of bladder control
Needing to leave the room
MAY ESCALATE TO: HAPPINESS (84), SATISFACTION (136)

CUES OF SUPPRESSED AMUSEMENT:
Clamping the lips together
Holding a hand up as if to say *No more!*
Shaking the head
Swallowing laughter
Wiping at the mouth
Covering the mouth, biting lips to hide a smile
A reddening of the face
Turning away to collect oneself
Confining a laugh to a snort
Pressing a fist against the lips

WRITER'S TIP: To create empathy for a character (including the antagonist), take the time to humanize them through their actions. Even the most unlikable person has a redeeming quality, so show it to the reader in a small, subtle way.

ANGER

DEFINITION: strong displeasure or wrath, usually aroused by a perceived wrong

PHYSICAL SIGNALS:
Flaring nostrils
Sweating
Holding elbows wide from the body, chest thrust out
Sweeping arm gestures
Handling objects or people roughly
A high chin
Noisy breathing
Legs that are planted wide
Baring one's teeth
Repetitive, sharp gestures (shaking a fist, etc.)
Cutting people off when they speak
Jerky head movements
Protruding eyes
Flexing the fingers or arm muscles
Cracking knuckles
Rolling up sleeves or loosening a collar
Eyes that are cold, hard, flinty
Entering another's personal space to intimidate
Jeers, taunts, a cutting wit
Tightness in the eyes or expression
Glaring
A reddening of the face
Lips that flatten or curl
Closed body posture (crossing the arms)
Nails biting into one's own palms
Pounding one's fists against thighs, table, a wall, etc.
Slamming doors, cupboards, or drawers
Punching, kicking, throwing things
Stomping or stamping
A vein that pulses, twitches, or becomes engorged
Laughter with an edge
A shaking or raised voice, yelling
Deepening one's tone
Deploying sarcasm, insulting others
Picking fights (verbal or physical)
Snapping at people

INTERNAL SENSATIONS:
Grinding one's teeth

Muscles quivering
Pulse speeding, heartbeat pounding
Body tensing
Heat flushing through the body
Sweating

MENTAL RESPONSES:
Irritability
Poor listening skills
Jumping to conclusions
Irrational reactions to inconsequential things
Demanding immediate action
Impetuosity
Taking inappropriate action or risks
Fantasizing violence

CUES OF ACUTE OR LONG-TERM ANGER:
Exploding over little things
Ulcers
Hypertension
Skin problems, such as eczema and acne
Damaging one's own property as a way to vent
Longer recovery time from surgeries, accidents, and other trauma
Cutting oneself
Road rage
Taking one's anger out on innocent bystanders
MAY ESCALATE TO: RAGE (120)

CUES OF SUPPRESSED ANGER:
Using a carefully controlled tone
Drawing in slow, steady breaths
False smiles
Passive-aggressive comments
Avoiding eye contact
Slanting the body away from the source of anger
Withdrawing from the conversation
Hiding one's hands and feet so clenching and twitching can't be seen
Excusing oneself for a brief time
Headache
Sore muscles and jaw

WRITER'S TIP: *Pay special attention to the events leading up to an emotional response. If the plotting feels contrived, the character's reaction will seem contrived as well.*

ANGUISH

DEFINITION: emotional or mental distress; acute suffering

PHYSICAL SIGNALS:
Manic pacing
Muttering
Rubbing the back of one's neck
Rocking back and forth
Tugging one's hair
Not eating or drinking
Visible sweating
Skin bunching around the eyes, a pained stare
Hands clenching into fists
Rubbing the wrists or wringing the hands
Restless fingers
Jumping at sounds
Grinding one's teeth
Clenching the jaw
Moving about, being unable to settle in one place
Muscles jumping under the skin
A corded neck
Curling one's toes
Repeatedly touching an object that symbolizes safety
Audible stress in one's voice and tone
Picking at lips, skin, or nails
Clutching at oneself
Shivering, moaning
Sobbing or weeping
Yelling or shouting
Checking and rechecking the time
Asking those in authority for updates
Shoulders that curl over the chest
Bringing one's legs up close to the body's core
Crying, wailing, begging for help
Turning away from others
Seeking corners in confined spaces
Rubbing the arms or legs
Beating at walls or surrounding objects

INTERNAL SENSATIONS:
Nausea
Sore muscles, stiffness, cramping
Pain in the back of the throat
Difficulty swallowing

Elevated body temperature

MENTAL RESPONSES:
Thinking irrationally
Praying, bargaining
Believing in anything that promises a positive outcome
Fixating on the source of suffering
A willingness to put oneself in harm's way for emotional relief

CUES OF ACUTE OR LONG-TERM ANGUISH:
Screaming for release
A gaunt appearance, wasting away
Premature aging
Posture that bends or crumples
Vomiting or dry heaves
Hyperventilation
Poor coloring, dark circles under the eyes
Wrinkles and sagging around the eyes and mouth
Alcohol, drug, or medication dependency
Bald patches
Facial tics or repetitive mannerisms (hair tugging, body rocking)
Cutting, scratching, or other self-destructive behaviors
Depression
Suicide
MAY ESCALATE TO: DESPERATION (52), DEPRESSION (48)

CUES OF SUPPRESSED ANGUISH:
Wincing
Gritting one's teeth
Uncontrolled shivering and hand tremors
Muscle tightness
Furtive movements
Hiding expressive gestures like hand wringing
Bitten nails, bleeding quicks
A downturned mouth or pinched lips
Attempting to hold back whimpers or moans
Heavy or shaky breathing
Minimal speaking (one-word answers, shaking or nodding the head)
Chain smoking
Drinking heavily
Sallow skin

WRITER'S TIP: Don't be afraid to challenge your character's morals. Putting them in situations that are outside their comfort zone will make them squirm, and the reader will too.

ANNOYANCE

DEFINITION: aggravation or mild irritation

PHYSICAL SIGNALS:
A pinched expression
Sighing heavily or with exaggeration
Statements suggesting impatience: *Here, I'll do it.*
Narrowing eyes
Crossed arms
Tapping a foot, fidgeting
Swatting at the air
Tics and tells (a throbbing forehead vein, fingering a collar)
Lips pressing into a white slash
Clenching the jaw
Grimacing, sneering, frowning
Complaining
Folding the arms across the chest
Hands that briefly clench
Making pointed suggestions to alleviate the annoyance
Tugging at clothing (jerking down a cuff, forcing a zipper up)
Cocking one's head and then shaking it
Raising one's eyebrows and giving a glassy stare
A gaze that flicks upward
Minutely shaking the head
Changing one's stance (shifting weight or position)
Propping the head up with a fist
Holding the head in the hands
Opening the mouth to criticize, then stopping short
Taking a deep breath and holding it in
Finger-tapping a tabletop
A smile that slips or appears forced
Snapping a pencil tip, using unnecessary force
Pacing
Light sarcasm
Asking a question that has a painfully obvious answer
A sharp tone
Speaking in short phrases
Visible tension in the neck, shoulders, and arms
Rigid posture, cords twanging in the neck
Rubbing the brow as if to ward off a headache
Avoiding the person or object of annoyance
Pressing a fist to the mouth

INTERNAL SENSATIONS:
A headache
Stiffness in the neck or jaw
Raised body temperature
Sensitivity to noise

MENTAL RESPONSES:
Berating thoughts
Straying attention
Thinking of an excuse to leave
Making unkind mental comparisons
Wishing to be somewhere else

CUES OF ACUTE OR LONG-TERM ANNOYANCE:
A reddening face
Rough handling of objects
Taking over someone else's job or duties
Grinding one's teeth
Throwing the hands up in a gesture of surrender
Stalking off to get some air
Shutting down, not speaking or responding
Pulling someone else into the situation to divert attention and allow one to exit
MAY ESCALATE TO: FRUSTRATION (78), ANGER (22)

CUES OF SUPPRESSED ANNOYANCE:
Nodding, but tightly, as if holding back from speaking an insult
Switching to another job to keep hands and thoughts busy
Attacking a task, diverting one's energy
Forcing oneself to remain in the presence of the annoyance
Faking interest, barely holding impatience at bay
Carefully controlling one's voice and tone
Focusing one's gaze elsewhere in an attempt to ignore

WRITER'S TIP: *Don't get caught up on the eyes to convey emotion. While eyes are often the first thing we notice in real life, they provide very limited options for description possibilities. Instead, dig deeper, showing how the character behaves through their body movement, actions and dialogue.*

ANTICIPATION

DEFINITION: hopeful expectation; to await eagerly

PHYSICAL SIGNALS:
Sweaty palms
Trembling hands
Crossing and uncrossing one's legs
Frantic planning for the event
List-making
Clasping one's hands to the chest
Being unable to think or talk about anything else
Fidgeting as if movement will make things go faster
Bouncing on one's toes
A bright-eyed look, engaging with others or the environment
Fussing with clothes, rearranging things
Waiting at a window, hovering at the door or by the phone
Checking and rechecking hair or makeup in a mirror
Gossiping with others, sharing excitement, giggling
Closing eyes and squealing
Jittering a foot against the floor
Covering one's face and then peeking
Biting one's lip
Fake swooning
Asking questions: *How long? When? What is it?*
Wetting the lips
Closing the eyes and sighing
Pacing
Rhythmic movements (swinging one's legs back and forth, etc.)
Obsessive clockwatching
Checking and rechecking email
Phoning or texting friends to talk about what's coming
Grabbing another person and saying *Tell me!*
Leaning in
Picking at food, too excited to eat
Begging someone for details, an answer, for a look at something

INTERNAL SENSATIONS:
A fluttery, empty feeling in the stomach
Breathlessness
A pounding heart
Tingling all over

MENTAL RESPONSES:
Daydreaming

A desire for perfection
Fearing that something will happen to screw things up
A lack of concentration
Imagining what will happen
Becoming self-critical (questioning clothing choices, abilities)

CUES OF ACUTE OR LONG-TERM ANTICIPATION:
Sleep loss
Frustration or impatience
Short-temperedness, irritability
Neglecting everything else (responsibilities, friends, family)
Fantasizing or building up the event far beyond its reality
Over-thinking (organizing every minute detail, etc.)
Going overboard in preparation (dressing over-the-top, etc.)
MAY ESCALATE TO: EXCITEMENT (74), JEALOUSY (102),
DISAPPOINTMENT (56)

CUES OF SUPPRESSED ANTICIPATION:
Sitting unnaturally still
Pressing one's lips together
Rubbing sweaty hands on one's clothes
Pretending to read a book or watch TV
A corded neck
Clamping one's hands tightly together
Avoiding conversation
Sneaking glances at a clock or doorway
Feigning boredom
Telling oneself that it doesn't matter
Acting interested in something else
Rolling one's shoulders and neck as if stiff
Changing the topic

WRITER'S TIP: *If a critique partner voices confusion over the emotional reaction of one of your characters, check to make sure the stimulus trigger is prominent. Showing the cause-effect relationship is vital when conveying authentic emotion.*

ANXIETY

DEFINITION: mental apprehension and unease; a sense of foreboding

PHYSICAL SIGNALS:
Rubbing the back of the neck
Crossing the arms, forming a barrier to others
Standing with one arm holding the other at the elbow
Clutching a purse, coat, or other object
Wringing one's hands
Twisting a watch or ring
Scratching
Hands repeatedly rising to touch one's face
Fingering a necklace
Rolling one's shoulders
Bouncing a foot
Glancing at the clock, phone, or doorway
Holding the stomach
Clutching one's hands
Rocking in place
Twisting one's neck as if sore
Biting at the lips or nails
Head shaking
Shifting, unable to get comfortable
Blowing out a series of short breaths to gain control
Digging in a purse or pocket to keep the hands busy
Becoming easily distracted
Adjusting clothes as if they chafe
Rubbing at one's hands
An inability to eat
Rubbing one's arms and looking around
Bouncing a curled knuckle against the mouth
A darting gaze
Increased awareness of one's environment
Starting at noises
Excessive swallowing
Repeatedly checking a phone for messages
Impatience
Praying

INTERNAL SENSATIONS:
Feeling too hot or too cold
Restless legs
Dizziness
A churning stomach

Increased thirst
Tingling in one's limbs
A tightening chest
Accelerated breathing
Feeling like one's insides are quivering

MENTAL RESPONSES:
Thinking about worst-case scenarios
Self blame
Seeking reassurance from others
Time feeling like it's slowing down
Discomfort in close spaces
Irrational worries
Replaying the events that caused the feeling

CUES OF ACUTE OR LONG-TERM ANXIETY:
Excessive sweating
A ragged appearance
Talking to oneself under the breath
Rocking in one's seat
Heart palpitations
Panic attacks
Hyperventilating
Emergence of fears, phobias, or OCD-like symptoms
MAY ESCALATE TO: FEAR (76), DESPERATION (52), PARANOIA (114)

CUES OF SUPPRESSED ANXIETY:
False smile
Avoiding conversation
Finding somewhere to be alone
Doing things to appear normal (ordering food but not eating it)
Feigning interest in something nearby
Closing one's eyes in an attempt to stay calm
Smoothing or stroking one's own hair as a soothing gesture

WRITER'S TIP: For each scene, identify the emotion you need to show and think in terms of three...what three ways have you reinforced the character's feelings through verbal and nonverbal communication?

CONFIDENCE

DEFINITION: having faith in one's own influence and ability

PHYSICAL SIGNALS:
Strong posture (shoulders back, chest out, chin high)
Walking with wide steps
Strong hygiene and personal grooming
Holding the hands loosely behind the back
Touching one's fingertips together (tapping, forming a steeple)
A gleam in one's eye, an inner light
Smiling, a playful grin
Winking or giving someone an easy nod
Keeping one's hands out of the pockets
Appearing relaxed (drumming fingers against a leg, humming)
Taking up space (legs spread wide, arms loose at the sides)
Approaching people with ease
Looking others directly in the eye
Arms swinging while walking
Choosing the middle, not the sides (be it a couch or a room)
Using exaggerated movements to draw attention to oneself
A booming laugh
A tilted-back head
Speaking boisterously
Offering witty commentary
Giving a half-shrug or a grin that conveys secret knowledge
Light-hearted teasing
Flirting
A strong handshake
Leaning back in a chair, hands behind the head
An easygoing manner
Stretching
Showing comfort in the close proximity of others
Initiating contact
Telling jokes, adding to or steering a conversation
Hosting events (getting the guys together for a football game)
Openness when dealing with people
Appearing unbothered by what others may think
Leaning in to talk or listen
Increased physical contact, becoming touchy-feely
Running hands through one's hair or flipping the hair back
Assuming a pose that draws attention to one's best attributes
Leading rather than following

INTERNAL SENSATIONS:
Relaxed muscles
Easy breaths
Lightness in the chest

MENTAL RESPONSES:
A sense of calm and ease
A positive outlook
Interest in whatever's going on

CUES OF ACUTE OR LONG-TERM CONFIDENCE:
Doing or saying things outside of the norm without anxiety or concern
Obsessively talking about an achievement or material object
Reacting with anger or jealousy if one's reputation is impugned
Bragging, showing off
MAY ESCALATE TO: SATISFACTION (136), SMUGNESS (144), CONTEMPT (38)

CUES OF SUPPRESSED CONFIDENCE:
Minimizing compliments
Modesty
Changing the topic to bring others into the spotlight
Downplaying one's own comfort level to make others feel better
Asking for opinions or advice

WRITER'S TIP: *It is natural to hold back or hide our true scope of emotions in the presence of others. When writing a conflicted protagonist, it is critical to show through action the emotion the character wants to convey to others while also expressing their true feelings to the reader.*

CONFLICTED

DEFINITION: experiencing opposing emotions

PHYSICAL SIGNALS:
Lips pressing together in a slight grimace
Increased swallowing or blinking
A smile that wavers
Gaze ping-ponging, avoiding direct eye contact
Start-and-stop gesturing (reaching then hesitating, changing direction mid-stride)
Broken dialogue, self-interruptions
Opening and closing the mouth
Struggling to find the right words
Voicing support, but with a tone that lacks enthusiasm
Becoming quieter, less animated
Scratching one's neck or cheek
Rubbing or pulling at an ear
Asking questions to gain more insight
Talking to others about similar experiences or situations
Gathering opinions on what others would do
Soft head shaking
A need to sit down and reflect
Rubbing or pinching the bottom lip
A pensive expression
Making a *Hmmm* noise in the throat
Tilting the head in a side-to-side rhythm
Pulling in and then slowly releasing a deep breath
Apologizing for one's lackluster reaction, citing mixed feelings
Requesting some time to digest everything
Tapping one's index finger against the lip
Brows pulling in
Looking downward
Rubbing at the middle of one's forehead, eyes closed
Voicing conflict: *This is a tough decision*
Voicing surprise: *Sorry, you caught me off guard*
Knees that bend, then straighten
A restless stance, pacing
Rubbing a hand through the hair
Smoothing one's clothes or touching items to keep the hands busy
Cancelling gestures (smiling while shaking the head, nodding and grimacing)
Holding one's elbow while the opposite hand makes a fist against the mouth
Blowing cheeks out, then swallowing the air or releasing it
Wrinkling the nose
Holding hands out and "weighing" them in the air
Rubbing a hand against the front of one's shirt (over heart)

Forcing enthusiasm because it's "the right thing to do"
Subdued or delayed reactions

INTERNAL SENSATIONS:
Headaches
A heaviness in the body
Tightness in the chest
A sinking feeling in the stomach
Loss of appetite

MENTAL RESPONSES:
Weighing the pros and cons
Researching or seeking information
Guilt toward those negatively affected by a final decision
Playing *What if?* to understand the repercussion of a situation
A need to verbalize the internal conflict
A desire to retreat and go somewhere quiet to think
An inability to focus on anything but the internal conflict
Drawing on moral beliefs to help one decide

CUES OF BEING CONFLICTED OVER THE LONG TERM:
A disheveled look (hair out of place, clothes rumpled)
Obsessive information-gathering, looking for the "key" solution
Stomach upset, poor diet, weight loss
Stress headaches
Difficulty sleeping
Loss of self confidence
Avoiding making any decisions at all
Hair loss
MAY ESCALATE TO: CONFUSION (36), OVERWHELMED (112),
FRUSTRATION (78), ANXIETY (30)

CUES WHEN SUPPRESSING THE FEELING OF BEING CONFLICTED:
Citing that one is not the ideal candidate to make the choice
Making excuses to avoid the situation
Suggesting that a break is needed to regroup
Making a joke to alleviate tension or lighten the mood
Giving a distracted nod to what's being said

WRITER'S TIP: *In scenes where information must be shared, characters should still be moving, acting, and revealing emotion to keep the pace flowing smoothly.*

CONFUSION

DEFINITION: a state of befuddlement or bafflement

PHYSICAL SIGNALS:
Difficulty completing a task
Fumbling
Using *um* and *uh* hesitations
Grimacing
Excessive swallowing
Scratching at one's cheek or temple
Rubbing the chin
Repeating back what was said as a question
Touching the base of the neck
Showing one's palms and shrugging
An uncertain tone
Increased difficulty in finding the right words
Body posture that loosens or collapses
Tilting one's head to the side and pursing the lips
Narrowed eyes
Stuttering
Head flinching back slightly
Trailing off when speaking
Running hands through the hair
Eyebrows that squish together
Pulling or tugging on an ear
Asking someone to repeat what was said
Gaze clouding, going distant
Rubbing one's forehead or eyebrows
Asking questions
Frowning
Biting one's lip
Rapid blinking
Hands touching the lips, mouth, face
Glancing around as if looking for answers
Wandering a short distance away before returning
Turning away to gather one's thoughts
A slight head shake
A mouth that opens but nothing comes out
Blowing out the cheeks, then releasing
A blank look, a slack expression
Staring down at the ground
Asking for affirmation: *Are you sure?*
Tapping a fist against the lips
Poking one's tongue into the cheek

Dry washing one's hands

INTERNAL SENSATIONS:
Rising body heat
Fluttering in the stomach
A tightening chest
Sweating
Feeling overheated

MENTAL RESPONSES:
Thoughts that freeze
Hoping for an interruption to delay answering
The mind racing, searching for answers

CUES OF ACUTE OR LONG-TERM CONFUSION:
Flight response
Failing grades
Loss of respect from others for unfinished or inaccurate work
Broken or unfulfilled promises
A lack of productivity
A loss of self esteem
MAY ESCALATE TO: OVERWHELMED (112), FRUSTRATION (78),
RESIGNATION (132), INSECURITY (98)

CUES OF SUPPRESSED CONFUSION:
Nodding or agreeing, to avoid attention
Waving a hand
False confidence
Assuring others that everything is under control
Smiling and nodding
Physical touches to reassure (a clap on the back or shoulder)
Fidgeting
Steering the conversation to a different topic
Launching into a flurry of activity
Making promises
Showing a sudden interest in other things
Visible sweating
Using "word filler" to stall for time

WRITER'S TIP: Men and women experience and express emotions differently. When writing a character of the opposite sex, get a second opinion if needed to ensure a character's reactions, thoughts, and feelings are authentic.

CONTEMPT

DEFINITION: a lack of reverence or respect; to hold in disregard

PHYSICAL SIGNALS:
Crossing one's arms, showing closed body posture
A downturned mouth
Head tilting away
Sneering
Head shaking
Mocking
Rolling the eyes
Using sarcasm
Gossiping
Snorting loudly
Buzzing the lips to be rude (blowing a raspberry)
Baiting the other person
Turning the body at an angle instead of facing the subject head-on
Walking away
Waving dismissively
Stiff posture
Refusing to respond or engage
Lowering the chin to look down on someone
Cold eyes
A pinched mouth
A hard, distinctive jaw line
Smirking as the subject speaks
Ugly laughter
Making jokes at another's expense
Flashing a cold smile to show insincerity
Spitting in the direction of the one provoking contempt
Sticking a tongue out
A wide stance, chest thrust out

INTERNAL SENSATIONS:
Rising blood pressure
A tightening in the chest
Stiffness in the neck and jaw
A roiling heat in the belly

MENTAL RESPONSES:
Negative thinking
Unkind observations
Mental insults
A desire to verbally tear down or hurt another person

38

Wanting to expose the subject's ignorance

CUES OF ACUTE OR LONG-TERM CONTEMPT:
Swearing and offering insults
Yelling, arguing
High blood pressure
A vein throbbing visibly in the forehead
Thoughts of violence
Angrily dismissing someone from one's presence
Leaving the room (excusing oneself, cutting a meeting short)
MAY ESCALATE TO: DISGUST (60), SCORN (138), ANGER (22)

CUES OF SUPPRESSED CONTEMPT:
Flushed skin
Biting at the cheek
Fidgeting
Pressing the lips together to keep from speaking
Dry washing one's hands
Purposefully not looking at the source
Feigning interest in something else
Turning away to ignore the source
Becoming non-responsive
Pushing on the diaphragm to keep the anger in
Leaning back, arms crossed
Moving away, creating personal distance

> **WRITER'S TIP:** *When revising, look for instances where emotions are NAMED. Nine times out of ten this indicates a lack of confidence that the emotion is shown clearly through thought, sensations and body language. Strong verbal and nonverbal cues negate the need to "explain" the emotion to the reader.*

CURIOSITY

DEFINITION: inquisitiveness; a desire for knowledge

PHYSICAL SIGNALS:
Tilting the head to the side
Raised eyebrows
Body posture that perks up
A slow smile that builds
Repeating a statement as a question
Leaning forward, sliding one's chair closer
Pausing to examine
Eyebrows furrowing and then releasing
Blinking
Gazing with focus
Shifting from casual conversation to pointed questions
A softened voice or tone that may contain wonder
Crossing one's arms while observing
Prying or snooping
Nose-wrinkling
Posing hypothetical questions
Lingering touches
Stopping to pay attention (a sudden halt, a fork pausing halfway to the mouth)
Straining to hear, shushing others to be quiet
Eavesdropping
Cupping an elbow with one hand while tapping the lips with the other
Pushing one's glasses up
Bending, kneeling, or squatting to get closer
Tilting one's body toward the source
Shuffling, creeping, or edging closer
Exploring the senses (smelling something new for the sake of knowing, etc.)
Verbally expressing interest: *Oh, look at that!* or *Isn't that amazing?*
Asking questions (who, what, when, where, and why)
Pulling on someone's sleeve to get them to join or follow
A still demeanor to aid in observation
Lips that are slightly parted
Nodding slowly
Poking or prodding at something

INTERNAL SENSATIONS:
Breaths that hitch or briefly stop
An increased pulse

MENTAL RESPONSES:
A need to know, touch, or understand

Forgetting what one was about to say or do
A compulsion to detour toward something new
Temporary cessation of worries, stress, or actions
A desire to investigate or experiment
Increased awareness of sensory information
Wonder or interest at how something works or why it's there

CUES OF ACUTE OR LONG-TERM CURIOSITY:
Fidgeting or tics
Hypersensitivity to the source of interest
Obsessive thoughts
Pointed or even rude questions
Snooping or sneaking about to satisfy the need to know
MAY ESCALATE TO: EAGERNESS (66), AMAZEMENT (18),
CONFLICTED (34)

CUES OF SUPPRESSED CURIOSITY:
Keeping one's eyes down
Holding the hands in the lap
Lack of eye contact
Providing an excuse to linger or move toward the source
Pretending to ignore or be unaware
A sidelong glance
Using one's hair to hide an interested glance
Feigning boredom

WRITER'S TIP: Smell triggers memory. Take advantage of this sense and build olfactory description into the scene. This will draw readers in and make them feel part of the action.

DEFEAT

DEFINITION: the feeling of having been mastered, conquered, or bested

PHYSICAL SIGNALS:
Chin lowering to one's chest
Hands that go limp
Holding one's palms up and out
Shaking the head
A lack of eye contact
Staring down at one's hands or feet
Going quiet or non-responsive
Weaving in place, a lack of balance
Agreeing for the sake of it
Arms hanging at one's sides
A long, low sigh
A thickened voice
Stumbling, knees hitching
Rubbing at the eyes, hiding redness or tears from others
Backing away
Cheeks that burn
A bobbing Adam's apple (thick swallows)
Hunched or rounded shoulders
Sagging posture
Hands hidden behind the back or in pockets
Chin tremors
Arms clutching one's body as if to hold it together
Lackluster movements
Toneless responses
Vacant eyes
Slumping into a chair
Holding one's head with the hands
A cracking voice

INTERNAL SENSATIONS:
Feeling a pulse in one's throat
Heart thudding dully in the chest
Wheezing breaths
Feeling like the head is spinning
Chest pain or numbness
A sour taste in one's mouth
A lack of energy
Tears or heat behind the eyelids
A painful lump in one's throat
Limbs that feel too heavy to lift or move

MENTAL RESPONSES:

A desire to flee or be alone
Shame
Worrying that others will feel let down or disappointed
Mental fatigue

CUES OF ACUTE OR LONG-TERM DEFEAT:

A quaking or trembling body
Uncontrollable tears
Pleading or begging
Collapsing, knees giving out
Self-loathing
MAY ESCALATE TO: RESIGNATION (132), DEPRESSION (48), SHAME (140), HUMILIATION (90)

CUES OF SUPPRESSED DEFEAT:

Shaking the head
False bravado
Trying to maintain eye contact
Demanding a rematch
Repeating the word *No*
Shouting, cursing
Laying the blame on others
Making accusations of cheating or underhandedness
A chin that juts sharply
A flinty gaze
Using anger to feed strength

WRITER'S TIP: *To reveal quieter emotions, try using contrast. For example, pairing a character with someone who is highly volatile will help their own milder body cues stand out clearly.*

DEFENSIVENESS

DEFINITION: resisting attack; defending against a perceived danger or threat

PHYSICAL SIGNALS:
Stepping back
Leaning away
Crossing the arms over one's chest
Rigid body posture
Squinting eyes
A lowering brow
Sucking the cheeks in
Shaking the head
Sputtering, gaping
Holding an object as a shield (a book, a folded jacket)
A darting gaze
Licking one's lips
Rapid blinking that leads to a wide-eyed look
Hands up, palms toward the aggressor
A fixed stare
Flipping one's hair in annoyance
A snort of dismissive laughter
Raising one's voice
Crossing the legs
Body shielding (turning at an angle)
Interrupting
Looking to others for backup
Blowing out a noisy breath
Going on the offensive and verbally attacking the accuser
Deflecting blame
Flinching, jerking back
Difficulty being articulate
Hand splaying across one's upper chest
Stiff neck, cords standing out
Chin lowering and pulling back against the neck
Wagging a finger, berating another for their accusations
Using sarcasm
Eye rolling
Rising color in one's cheeks
Visible sweating
Dragging others into the situation for support
Verbalizing disappointment or denial
A voice that hardens over the course of an argument
Jerky movements, a loss of fluidity to actions
Excessive swallowing

INTERNAL SENSATIONS:
Raised blood pressure
A pounding heartbeat that grows loud in the ears
Dry mouth
A body that feels hot
Intense thirst
The stomach tightening and hardening

MENTAL RESPONSES:
Scrambling thoughts, trying to diffuse the situation
Anger, shock
Feeling betrayed
Sifting memories for evidence (to support innocence or challenge accusations)

CUES OF ACUTE OR LONG-TERM DEFENSIVENESS:
Eyes darting for an exit or escape (flight response)
Shouting
Bringing up past examples when one supported the accuser or saved the day
Citing an opponent's shortcomings
Increasing one's personal space
Storming away
MAY ESCALATE TO: ANGER (22), FEAR (76)

CUES OF SUPPRESSED DEFENSIVENESS:
Maintaining an even tone
Offering a fake smile
A forcibly calm demeanor
Changing the subject
Denial (shrugging, forcing a laugh)
Calmly stating that one doesn't need to prove anything
Not leaving or walking away, despite discomfort
Attempting to reason through facts, not emotion

WRITER'S TIP: Choose each setting with deliberate care. Each location should symbolize something to your main character, and have an impact (positive or negative) on their psyche coming into the scene.

DENIAL

DEFINITION: a refusal to acknowledge truth or reality

PHYSICAL SIGNALS:
Verbal disagreement
Backing away
Vigorous head shaking
Waving someone off
Dialogue in the negative: *Don't blame me* or *I had nothing to do with it*
Speaking emphatically with finger pointing or other hard gestures
Raising one's palms
Shrugging
Tucking in the upper lip
Arms crossing one's chest, closed body posture
Placing a hand against the breastbone
A slackened mouth, displaying shock
Speaking rapidly, not letting others get a word in
Rationalizing or justifying
Shuffling backward
Speaking slowly, stretching out words: *What? No way!*
Leaning back, creating space
Warding someone or something off
Raised eyebrows
Widening eyes
Raising one's voice
Emphatically saying *No*
Slanting the body away from an accuser
Questioning someone's source or the facts
Making an "X" motion with one's hands
Eye contact dropping (if one is unsure or lying)
Choppy responses, short sentences
Sweating
Staring down at one's hands

INTERNAL SENSATIONS:
Mouth going dry
A lump forming in one's throat
Feeling heavy or numb
Heat rising behind the eyelids
Tingling in the stomach

MENTAL RESPONSES:
Replaying past events in order to understand
Thoughts centering on the facts of the situation

Brain scrambling to find a logical excuse (if lying)
Anger or hurt at being put in this situation

CUES OF ACUTE OR LONG-TERM DENIAL:
Blaming others
Pleading, crying, begging to be believed
Becoming closed-minded, refusing to listen
Wanting to be left alone
MAY ESCALATE TO: DEFENSIVENESS (44), HURT (92), GUILT (82), ANGER (22), CONFLICTED (34)

CUES OF SUPPRESSED DENIAL:
Refusing to argue or respond to an accusation
Steady eye contact
Explaining that one is not in denial
Voicing *We'll see* comments
Supplying reasons to convey that a viewpoint is invalid
Repeating the truth as one sees it and sticking to it
A steady, even tone

WRITER'S TIP: Make a list of your body language crutches (frowning, smiling, shrugging, head shaking, etc.). Use your word processor's search and replace feature to highlight these so you can pinpoint where the emotional description needs some freshening up.

DEPRESSION

DEFINITION: a state of withdrawal; extreme sadness and reduced vitality

PHYSICAL SIGNALS:
A gaunt appearance
Notable weight loss or gain
Eyes that blink infrequently
Wet or red eyes
Staring down at one's hands
Becoming non-reactive to stimulus or noise
Laying in bed with no motivation to get up
Saggy posture, bent neck
Head resting on one's hand
Tangled hair, overlong nails, and other signs of letting oneself go
Wearing the same clothes day after day
Shuffling steps
Lethargic hand movements
Obsession with an object that represents loss (a photo or trinket)
Crying
A vacant stare
Making excuses
A downturned mouth
Lines in the face, a slack expression
Dark circles under one's eyes
An inability to sleep
Sleeping too much
Poor eating habits
A tone that lacks strength or vitality
An unclean home, room, or office space
Ignoring phone calls or visitors
Premature aging (wrinkles, tired eyes, gray or white hair)
Illness
Having no interest in hobbies
Failing grades at school, lack of success at work
Choosing isolation
Dropping out of activities and moving away from friendships
Picking at food or finding food tasteless
Being unable to focus on tasks (work, school, home life)
Forgetting appointments, conversations, and meetings
Bulky or dull clothing choices
Non-responsiveness to others, even family
Poor conversation skills
Body odor

INTERNAL SENSATIONS:
A hollowness in one's chest
A slow pulse
Aches and pains
Shallow breathing
Fatigue

MENTAL RESPONSES:
Focusing inward
Desiring to live in the past or be alone
Poor observation skills
Obsessive thoughts
A negative outlook
An inability to concentrate
Losing track of time
Thoughts of self-harm
Bleak observations about the world and the people in it
An aversion to noise, crowds, and stressful situations

CUES OF ACUTE OR LONG-TERM DEPRESSION:
Eating disorders
Manic behavior (hair pulling, OCD, paranoia)
Thoughts of suicide
Suicide attempts
Addiction to medication
Hoarding
MAY RELATE TO: NOSTALGIA (110), REGRET (122), SADNESS (134)

CUES OF SUPPRESSED DEPRESSION:
Slight pauses before reacting
Emotional displays that seem forced or false
Heavy self-medicating or drinking
Wearing false, overly bright smiles
Pretending to be ill to avoid social situations and people
Lying

WRITER'S TIP: It isn't enough to show emotion; a writer needs to make the reader feel it. Think about the core visceral sensations you experience when feeling strong emotion, and if appropriate, utilize them to convey a similar experience to the reader.

DESIRE

DEFINITION: to covet, wish, or long for
NOTE: the object of desire can be a person, a thing, or an intangible (prestige, acceptance, etc.)

PHYSICAL SIGNALS:
Lips parting
Firm eye contact
Hands moistening
Stroking one's arm as a surrogate for the object of desire
Mirroring the object's movements (if a person)
Trembling
Lowering one's voice when speaking
Leaning in or forward
Moving closer to erase distance
Relaxing one's posture
Facing the object straight on
Eyes shining, glossing over, and softening
Slightly parting the legs
Muscles losing tension
Frequent touching of the face and lips
Hands clenching briefly, then releasing
Becoming inarticulate
Skin flushing
Increased swallowing
The tongue darting out to touch or lick the lips
Knees loosening and feeling weak
Responding immediately when called upon
Touching or holding the object close
A slow smile that builds
Subconsciously thrusting out one's chest
Lifting one's chin to expose the neck
Holding in a breath
Stuttering or stammering
A lingering touch, brushing up against the object
Touching or stroking one's own throat

INTERNAL SENSATIONS:
A strong awareness of one's own heartbeat
The sensation of being flooded with warmth
The mouth becoming moist, increased saliva
A sensation of hair raising on one's arms and nape
Fingers aching or tingling with the need to touch

Quickening breath or breathlessness
Hypersensitivity to touch and texture
Fluttering or even mild pain in the chest
Light-headedness
A shifting feeling near the heart, a pang
A shiver that brings pleasure
Nerve endings that stir and tingle
Bodily cravings of being touched by the object (person)

MENTAL RESPONSES:
Preoccupation with the object's scent
Focusing on the object's most desirable qualities
Tuning out distractions in order to fixate on the object or want
A desire to erase all distance
A need to touch and explore
Daydreaming or fantasizing about the object
A determination to have or own
Impatience
A loss of inhibitions
Setting goals to obtain the object
Taking opportunities or meeting challenges to prove one's worth
Wanting to care for and put the object's needs first

CUES OF ACUTE OR LONG-TERM DESIRE:
Bumping, pushing, or shoving to get closer
A willingness to endure suffering or hardship to obtain the object
Not caring what others think or feel
Obsessive thoughts
Centering all aspects of one's life on being with the object
Neglecting friends, family, work, and other interests
Fixation on self-improvement, education, or goals leading to achievement
Shedding bad habits or flaws to appease or impress
MAY ESCALATE TO: ADORATION (14), LOVE (106), DETERMINATION (54), ENVY (72), JEALOUSY (102)

CUES OF REPRESSED DESIRE:
Glancing away for a brief time
Feigning interest in something else
Making a display of engaging in conversation with others
Examining or pretending to consider other objects
Smiling at other objects
Forcing a slow gait rather than rushing to be with the object

WRITER'S TIP: *Emotion should always lead to decision making, either good or bad, that will propel the story forward.*

DESPERATION

DEFINITION: a state of hopelessness that leads to rashness

PHYSICAL SIGNALS:
Feverish, over-bright eyes
A darting gaze
Quick movements
An inability to sleep or eat
Finger twitches, compulsive and repetitive movements
A herky-jerky walk
Reaching or touching in hopes of gaining help or favor
Facing danger head-on
Acting in ways that push the limits of endurance
Pacing
Anxiously muttering to oneself
Grabbing fistfuls of one's hair and pulling
A pained stare
An emotion-choked voice
Fluttery hand movements
Moaning
Rocking in place
Bargaining
Shaking, trembling
Curling the arms over the head
Hugging one's shoulders, chin resting on the chest
Stiff neck, strained forearms
Eyes that appear wet
Teeth biting down on the bottom lip
Wringing one's hands
Shoulders curling, a bent spine
Shaking one's head in denial
Protective posture (chin to chest, arms holding the body tight)
Dragging nails down the cheeks
Rubbing one's upper arms for comfort
A shaking voice
Sweating profusely

INTERNAL SENSATIONS:
Racing heartbeat
A dry mouth
A sore throat from pleading, crying, begging
A heightened level of pain resistance
Tightness or pain in the chest
Excessive or manic energy

MENTAL RESPONSES:

Constant planning and obsessing
Irrational thinking, poor judgment
A willingness to do anything
Ignoring the law or society's values
Casting morality and good judgment aside
Sacrificing others or lesser goals, desires, and needs if necessary
Disregarding another's feelings if they conflict with one's goal

CUES OF ACUTE OR LONG-TERM DESPERATION:

Crying, sobbing, wailing
Screaming
Beating one's fists against something to the point of injury
Kneeling
Pleading, abasing, or disregarding personal worth or pride
Extreme risk taking
Offering an exchange: *Take me instead* or *I'll go, you stay*
Pushing past one's limits to find needed strength
Refusing to be persuaded
MAY ESCALATE TO: TERROR (154), DREAD (64), ANGER (22), DETERMINATION (54)

CUES OF SUPPRESSED DESPERATION:

Holding oneself tight
Believing a lie if it offers hope
Fidgeting
Retreating internally to cope, shutting the world out
Difficulty sitting still
Clock-watching
Reassuring others
Fixing one's hair and clothes to appear unaffected
Taking advantage of a distraction (watching a movie, TV)
Curling hands into tight fists

WRITER'S TIP: *Clothing choices are individual and project an image of one's personality. When creating unique emotional body language, think about how a character's clothing can be utilized to reveal their insecurities or vanities and show feelings of self-worth.*

DETERMINATION

DEFINITION: firm intention on achieving a goal; decisiveness

PHYSICAL SIGNALS:
Being the first to speak
Moving into someone's personal space
Using articulate words and short, strong sentences
A steady, lower-pitched voice
A furrowing brow
Tight muscles
Alert gaze
A set jaw
Strong eye contact
A curt nod
Forming hands into a steeple
Mirroring the leader's movements
Using affirmative words: *Yes* and *I will*
Pressing the lips together
Tightening fists
Organizing one's things, being prepared
Standing solidly, at the ready
Planting one's feet in a wide stance
Leaning in, hand on one knee
A high chin, neck exposed
Pushing up one's sleeves
Shoulders pushing back
Strong posture
Precise movements
Sharp hand movements (jabbing a finger for emphasis, etc.)
A fast-paced stride
Asking pointed questions
Straightened legs, knees uncrossed
Thrusting the chest out
Offering a firm handshake
Inhaling deeply through the nose, then exhaling through the mouth
Exuding calm and focus
Practicing a skill
Making preparations or conditioning the body
Studying or gathering information
Accepting criticism to improve

INTERNAL SENSATIONS:
A fluttery feeling in the chest
Increased internal temperature and heartbeat

Muscles tightening in readiness

MENTAL RESPONSES:
Planning for obstacles and strategizing ways to overcome them
Mentally encouraging oneself to succeed
Active listening
An acute sense of purpose
Ignoring distractions or discomforts
Extreme mental focus on the objective
Running through what one must say or do
Dismissing negative thoughts
Setting goals

CUES OF ACUTE OR LONG-TERM DETERMINATION:
Conditioning for the task in advance
Muscle clenching along the jaw line
Headaches
Muscle strain
Ignoring pain, stress, or any outside elements
Sacrificing what is needed to achieve the desired result
MAY ESCALATE TO: HOPEFULNESS (88), CONFIDENCE (32)

CUES OF SUPPRESSED DETERMINATION:
Purposely adopting a languid pose
Feigning disinterest
Meaningless gestures (scrutinizing cuticles, checking for split ends)
Placing one's hands in one's pockets
Engaging in banter or non-threatening conversation
Benign questions
Yawning
Shrugging
Laughing or making jokes meant to disarm
A lack of eye contact
Closing one's eyes as if relaxed or dosing

WRITER'S TIP: *Never underestimate the power of texture. The way an object feels against the skin can create a powerful reaction (positive or negative) and add to the reader's emotional experience.*

DISAPPOINTMENT

DEFINITION: a state of dismay or dissatisfaction; feeling let down

PHYSICAL SIGNALS:
Lowering one's head
Lips pressing tight
Shoulders dropping or slumping
A hunched posture
Looking up with hands raised in the *why me?* position
Collapsing onto a chair or bench
Weaving slightly
A bitter smile
A heavy sigh
Covering one's face with one's hands
Breaking eye contact
Bending the neck forward
Slowly shaking one's head
Tilting the chin down and frowning
Making a noise in one's throat
Swallowing hard
Sagging against a door or wall, reaching out to steady oneself
Dropping the head, eyes closed
Stumbling mid-stride
Face going slack and paling slightly
The mouth falling open
Pressing hands to one's temples
Weaving hands into the hair and pulling
Frowning
A stony expression
Watering eyes that display an inward focus
Wincing
Looking around in confusion or shock
Attempting to hide (covering the head, ducking one's chin)
Restless fiddling
Hands fluttering like they've lost track of what they should be doing
Feet shuffling, kicking at the ground
Rubbing at the back of one's neck
A voice that drops or goes quiet
Whispering *No* or cursing under the breath
Biting or chewing at the lip
Clutching oneself (gripping the elbows, rubbing the arms)
Pressing a hand to the abdomen
Slinking away (flight response)

INTERNAL SENSATIONS:
A heart that feels like it's shrinking
A clenching stomach
Sudden onset of nausea
A tightening chest
Breaths that hitch
A heaviness in the body

MENTAL RESPONSES:
Negativity
A feeling of dread or hopelessness
Defeatist thoughts about oneself
Wanting to be alone
Feeling worthless

CUES OF ACUTE OR LONG-TERM DISAPPOINTMENT:
Berating oneself
Wallowing (drinking too much, listening to depressing songs)
Obsessing over why things happened the way they did
An inability to move on
MAY ESCALATE TO: DEPRESSION (48), DEFEAT (42), RESENTMENT (130), ANGER (22)

CUES OF SUPPRESSED DISAPPOINTMENT:
A slight lip press
Dropping the shoulders, then hitching them up again
Offering false cheer, a weak smile
Comforting others
Citing a backup plan or listing more options
Making promises
Clasping one's hands in one's lap
Congratulating the victor

WRITER'S TIP: *Characters experiencing raw emotion often react without thinking—either through dialogue or action. Rash behavior creates the perfect storm for increased tension and conflict.*

DISBELIEF

DEFINITION: withholding belief; a refusal to see the truth

PHYSICAL SIGNALS:
Mouth slackening
Eyes widening
Looking down or away
Rubbing at an eyelid or brow
Being at a loss for words
Turning away and covering the mouth
Expression blanching, going pale
Asking *Are you sure?* type questions
Scratching one's jaw
A shake of the head
Rubbing absently at the arms
Verbalizing shock: *Are you kidding?* or *Impossible!*
Moving back slightly, increasing one's personal space
Showing one's palms
Lifting a single eyebrow
Cocking the head
An unfocused gaze
Rapid blinking
Running hands through one's hair
Gaping, stuttering, mouth opening and closing
Hands dropping to one's sides
Posture slumping slightly
Neck bending forward
Hands carving through one's hair, holding it back and then releasing
Pulling glasses down and looking over the rims
Openly staring
Covering one's ears
Repeating *No* and other negatives: *It's not true!*
Folding the arms over the stomach
Staring at one's palms as if they hold the answers
Jiggling, tugging, or tapping the earlobe
Doing a double take
Waving something off

INTERNAL SENSATIONS:
A tingling in one's chest
A hardening or clenching stomach
A small intake of breath (gasp)
Lightheadedness
Restricted breathing

MENTAL RESPONSES:
Making an immediate moral judgment (either good or bad, wrong or right)
Thoughts scrambling to understand
Attempting to reason or glean more information
Pretending to have misheard

CUES OF ACUTE OR LONG-TERM DISBELIEF:
A restless stance
Arguing
Walking away
Voicing the emotion over and over: *I just can't believe this*
Difficulty speaking, choppy responses
Holding a hand up to ward off the truth
Demanding those with influence do something to change the outcome
Closed body posture (arms creating a barrier across the chest)
MAY ESCALATE TO: DENIAL (46), ANGER (22), OVERWHELMED (112), RESIGNATION (132)

CUES OF SUPPRESSED DISBELIEF:
Changing the topic
A nervous laugh
Making excuses
Supporting the outcome, acting like one was "in the know" all along
Reassuring others of one's belief, commitment, etc.
Asking questions to glean information without giving away disbelief
Throat clearing
Coughing, pretending a drink went down wrong
Avoiding eye contact
Offering fake platitudes: *Interesting* or *Well, that's good then.*

WRITER'S TIP: *While melodrama is usually a bad idea in fiction, it can be used effectively to characterize an over-the-top character.*

DISGUST

DEFINITION: an aversion, usually to something distasteful; revulsion

PHYSICAL SIGNALS:
A curling lip
An open mouth, the tongue pushing slightly forward
Wrinkling one's nose
Flinching, recoiling
Swallowing hard
Leaning back
Stroking the throat and grimacing
Turning one's back to the source
Eyes that appear cold, dead, flat
Refusing to look
Shaking one's head, muttering
Walking away to regain composure
Toes curling up
Pulling up a collar to cover the mouth and nose
Averting one's gaze
Spitting, coughing or throwing up
Hands up, backing away with a shudder
Repeating what someone has said, purposely devoid of all emotion
Dry washing the hands
Pressing a fist against the mouth and puffing out the cheeks
Rubbing at one's exposed forearms
Covering the mouth
Making a choking noise in the throat
Jerking away from contact, or even the suggestion of contact
Pressing hands against the stomach
Demanding that someone stop speaking or desist what they are doing
Violently rolling shoulders as if one's own clothing is creating discomfort
Using a purse or jacket to create a shield
Shunning or offering evasive answers
Eyebrows lowering and pinching together
Pressing one's knees together
Narrowing one's stance, bringing the feet together
A face that blanches
Rubbing at one's nose or mouth
Dry heaving
Cringing away from the source
An expression that appears pained

INTERNAL SENSATIONS:
A choking or uncomfortable swallow

Excessive saliva, a need to spit
A sour or bitter tang in the mouth
Nausea or a heaving stomach
Burning in the throat
Skin tightening (crawling flesh sensation)

MENTAL RESPONSES:
A compulsion to flee
Feeling unclean
Wishing to be somewhere else
The mind replaying what was seen in agonizing detail

CUES OF ACUTE OR LONG-TERM DISGUST:
Focusing on cleanliness (showering, rubbing skin raw)
Hyper-protectiveness of personal space
Acting jumpy or jittery when near the source
Becoming non-responsive, less verbal
An intense need to flee the source
MAY ESCALATE TO: SCORN (138), FEAR (76), ANGER (22)

CUES OF SUPPRESSED DISGUST:
Offering a watery smile while maintaining a safe distance
Forcing oneself to come closer
Maintaining eye contact, no matter how difficult
Waving a hand as if something doesn't matter
Biting the lip
Slowly walking closer, but keeping arms close to the body
Standing away and reaching in with one hand
Hesitating
Heavy, jerky movements
A frozen smile

WRITER'S TIP: *With extreme emotions that trigger an immediate fight-or-flight response, it's important to know which "side" fits best with your character's personality. All actions should line up with this choice.*

DOUBT

DEFINITION: to lack confidence in or consider unlikely

PHYSICAL SIGNALS:
Brows drawing closer, face tightening
Looking down or away
Avoiding eye contact
Pressing the lips together
Shuffling one's feet
Shoving hands in pockets
Throat clearing
Thumbing the ear
Expressing concern
Checking and rechecking one's appearance
Delaying tactics (suggesting time to review options, etc.)
Pauses, *ums*, or other conversation fillers
Taking a slight step back
Lingering at the edge of a group or event
Biting one's cheek
Declining an offer of support
Running hands through the hair
Pulling or tugging at one's clothes
A smile that appears tight
A hesitating nod
Rocking on one's heels, pretending to study the floor
Cocking the head while raising the eyebrows
Swallowing more than usual
Tipping one's head side to side, weighing an idea or choice
Tapping the fingers together
Slightly clenched fists
A deep, weighted sigh
Pursing the lips
Shrugging
Shaking the head
Asking for assurances or clarification
Arguing or questioning
Citing possible repercussions
Rubbing the back of the neck
Fiddling with a ring or button to avoid eye contact
Putting a hand over the face, closing the eyes
Drawing in breath, then releasing it
Tactfully offering alternative suggestions
Hesitation (accepting a leaflet with reluctance, etc.)
Crossing the arms or legs

INTERNAL SENSATIONS:
A slight heaviness or quiver in the stomach

MENTAL RESPONSES:
Worrying over the current path
Looking ahead to possible collateral damage
Searching for ideas on how to circumvent the situation
Dredging up evidence in order to sway opinions
Hoping or praying it will work out

CUES OF ACUTE OR LONG-TERM DOUBT:
Avoiding speaking or agreeing openly
Sharing a look with an ally, raising the eyebrows to convey a message
Wincing as others rally behind a weak solution
MAY ESCALATE TO: WORRY (162), DISBELIEF (58), UNEASE (158)

CUES OF SUPPRESSED DOUBT:
Fidgeting in a chair
Coughing as one agrees or supports a doubtful decision or stance
Mimicking confidence (straightening, speaking in a booming voice)
Lying or misleading others
Making excuses for not agreeing immediately
Reassuring others of loyalty, commitment, etc.
Offering to handle the problem instead
Delaying verbal support

WRITER'S TIP: When steering your character through scenes that allow for emotional growth, don't forget to also provide setbacks. The path to enlightenment isn't smooth for anyone, including our characters.

DREAD

DEFINITION: a nearly overpowering fear to face or meet; a strong desire to avoid a future event or circumstance

PHYSICAL SIGNALS:
Holding the stomach as if pained
Clutching arms to one's chest
Shoulders curling forward, caving the chest in
A bent neck
Leaning back or away from the source of discomfort
Dragging footsteps
Making excuses to leave
A quiet voice, offering one-word responses
Hunched posture and a drooping head
Clasping one's knees tightly together
Avoiding eye contact
Turning the torso, shielding it
Lifting the shoulders as if to hide one's neck
Sweating
Rocking slightly
Hands that tremble
Seeking the safety of darkness, an exit, etc.
Holding one's elbows tightly against sides
A downward gaze, using the hair as a shield
Making oneself appear smaller
Huddling in the corner, behind, or against something
Flinching or cringing
Heavy footsteps
Uncontrollable whimpering
Increased swallowing
Arms crossing the stomach in a protective huddle
Rubbing and twisting one's hands, spinning rings or bracelets
Scratching at the skin, picking or biting at nails
Clutching comfort items (a necklace charm, phone, etc.)
Dragging the palms down one's pant legs
Chewing at one's lips or inner cheek and making them bleed
A pale or sickly complexion

INTERNAL SENSATIONS:
A rolling stomach
Heavy or sluggish heartbeat
Chills
Cold fingers
Tingling in the chest

64

A weighted chest
Difficulty breathing
A sour taste in the mouth
Ache in the back of the throat
Difficulty swallowing
Dizziness
Shakiness in the limbs

MENTAL RESPONSES:
Thoughts of escape
Wanting to hide
Wishing time would speed up
An inability to see a positive outcome
The need to check for danger overriding the need to hide

CUES OF ACUTE OR LONG-TERM DREAD:
Shaking, shuddering
Jumping at sounds
Teeth chattering
Weeping
Seeking any excuse to avoid what is to come
Hyperventilating
Bargaining, pleading
Anxiety attack
MAY ESCALATE TO: ANGUISH (24), TERROR (154)

CUES OF SUPPRESSED DREAD:
Acting like one is simply feeling under the weather
Attempting to escape via distraction (TV, book, music)
Focusing thoughts to keep fear from taking over
Keeping still

> **WRITER'S TIP:** *Maintain an overall perspective of the book's emotional range. A strong manuscript will always expose the reader to several contrasting emotional experiences that fit within the context of the protagonist's growth.*

EAGERNESS

DEFINITION: enthusiasm for what is to come

PHYSICAL SIGNALS:
Leaning forward
Eyes that glow
Rushing one's words
Speaking in a bubbly or loud tone
Rapt attention, nodding
Using excitable language
Agreeability to whatever is suggested
Fiddling with an object to keep the hands busy
Squeezing the hands at one's sides
Strong eye contact
Talking over others
Raising a hand immediately to be called on
Asking questions, requesting information
Rubbing the hands together
Leaning forward with a hand on the knee
Sitting at the edge of a chair
Allowing others into one's personal space
Licking one's lips, smiling
Feet pointing forward
Shoulders straight and back
Animated gesturing
Bouncing on one's toes
Moving, fidgeting, pacing
Blowing out a long breath and smiling
Eyes wide, rounded, with very few blinks
Hands clutched together
Head up, alert
A fast walk, jog, or run
Sharing a look or wink with another
Clambering closer to a group or event
Whispering in hushed, excitable tones
Scuffing a chair closer to the table
Arriving early
Quirking an eyebrow and smiling
Friendliness, even with those not in one's own social circle
Pulling or prodding others to hurry up

INTERNAL SENSATIONS:
Fluttery stomach
Increased heartbeat

66

An expanding feeling in the chest
Breathlessness
Adrenaline causing alertness

MENTAL RESPONSES:
Focused listening
Strong organization and preparedness
An inability to concentrate on anything else
Desiring to share and include others
Losing all inhibitions
Positive outlook and thinking
A willingness to take on responsibility, to help or lead

CUES OF ACUTE OR LONG-TERM EAGERNESS:
Preparing early, often hours or days before needed
Planning or obsessing over every detail
Seeking perfection
Hurrying or rushing to make things happen quicker
MAY ESCALATE TO: EXCITEMENT (74), IMPATIENCE (94)

CUES OF SUPPRESSED EAGERNESS:
Clamping the hands in the lap
Tight muscles
Forcing oneself to sit still
Slowing one's speech, concentrating on being articulate
A series of deep breaths
Taking up a task or chore to pass the time
Feigning disinterest by adopting a loose and relaxed posture
Making a slight detour as a ruse

WRITER'S TIP: *To generate friction in dialogue, give the participants opposing goals. A heightened emotional response is the natural result of not getting what one needs.*

ELATION

DEFINITION: in high spirits; a state of euphoria or exhilaration

PHYSICAL SIGNALS:
High color, a flushed appearance
A smile or grin that cannot be contained
Laughing
Squealing, screaming, shouting, whooping, hollering
Falling to one's knees
Jumping up and down
Talking over one another, babbling
Holding arms up in a "Victory V"
Head tipping back, turning one's face to the sky
Running a victory lap
A beaming face, strong color and sheen
Embracing others
Dancing in place
Whooping loudly
Not caring what others think, a lack of self-consciousness
Enjoying communal happiness, feeling part of the crowd
Repeating words over and over: *Wow!* or *This is amazing!*
Flinging out the arms and legs, taking a wide stance
Thrusting the chest out
Eyes wide and glowing
Grabbing at the sides of the head in an "I can't believe it" gesture
High energy, a bouncing walk or run, skipping
Hugging, kissing, or other displays of affection
Breaking out into a run
Happy tears, shining cheeks
Throwing something into the air—a hat, books, confetti, helmet
Sweating
Thrusting a fist into the sky

INTERNAL SENSATIONS:
Warmth radiating throughout the body
Racing heartbeat, drumming in the chest
Feeling ultra-awake, rejuvenated by adrenaline

MENTAL RESPONSES:
Thoughts scatter, too excited to think straight
Wanting to be surrounded by family and friends
Feeling vindicated for the effort, sacrifice, or hard work
Revisiting the hurdles leading to this moment
Gratitude to those who helped make this possible

CUES OF ACUTE OR LONG-TERM ELATION:

Tears streaming down the face

Loss of motor control

Trembling muscles

Sinking to the ground, exhausted

Breathlessness

Losing one's voice from screaming or shouting

Speechlessness

MAY ESCALATE TO: SATISFACTION (136), PRIDE (118), GRATITUDE (80)

CUES OF SUPPRESSED ELATION:

A grin that can't be contained no matter how hard one tries

Bottling up one's breaths to try and calm down

Self-hugging to contain the feeling

Closing the eyes and covering the mouth

Quivering with the effort of controlling oneself

Looking down to hide a grin

WRITER'S TIP: Make a list of the body parts you incorporate when expressing emotion. Are there ones you don't use at all? Challenge yourself to come up with a unique cue by using one of these "missing" parts, and substitute it for a gesture that is overused.

EMBARRASSMENT

DEFINITION: a lack of composure due to self-conscious discomfort

PHYSICAL SIGNALS:
A flush that creeps across the cheeks
Visible sweating
The body freezing in place
Grimacing or swallowing
Ears that turn red
The chin dipping down
The chest caving
A bent spine
Hands curling around one's middle
Feet shuffling
Clearing the throat
Coughing
Covering oneself (crossing the arms, closing a jacket)
Pulling at the collar
Rubbing the back of the neck
Wincing
Covering the face with hands
Cringing or shaking
Fidgeting, squirming
Stuttering, stammering
Flinching away from touches
A weakened voice
Speechlessness
Toes curling up
Knees pulling together
Arms tucking in at the sides
Sliding down in a chair
Looking down, unable to meet someone's eyes
Shoulders slumping or curling forward
Responding with anger (shoving, punching)
Gritting one's teeth, pressing the lips tight
Shoving hands in pockets
Fiddling with shirt sleeves
Hiding behind a book
Shielding (having a death grip on a purse)
A walk that accelerates into a sprint
Using hair to hide one's face
Glancing about for help, an exit, or escape
Tugging a hat down low or pulling a hood over the head
A trembling chin

INTERNAL SENSATIONS:
Excessive swallowing
Lightheadedness
A tingling that sweeps up the back of the neck and across the face
A tightening chest
Stomach hardening or dropping with a manifestation of dread
The face, neck, and ears feeling impossibly hot
Rushed breathing
A rapid heartbeat

MENTAL RESPONSES:
A compulsion to flee (fight-or-flight)
Muddied or panicked thoughts
A disconnect where the mind struggles with belief: *This can't be happening!*
Thoughts searching for a solution

CUES OF ACUTE OR LONG-TERM EMBARRASSMENT:
Crying
Running from the room or situation
Plummeting self-esteem
Fear of public speaking or being on display
Withdrawing from groups, activities, and social interaction
Loss of appetite
Obsessing about the embarrassing event, reliving it
Poor sleep
Weight loss
MAY ESCALATE TO: HUMILIATION (90), DEPRESSION (48), REGRET (122), SHAME (140)

CUES OF SUPPRESSED EMBARRASSMENT:
Pretending to not have heard or seen
Intensely concentrating on something else, actively ignoring others
A fake smile
Trying to laugh it off
Changing the topic in any way possible
Lying
Deflecting attention and assigning blame to another

WRITER'S TIP: Be wary of showing emotion too readily through the act of crying. In real life, it takes a lot to reach a tearful state and so it should be the same for our characters.

ENVY

DEFINITION: resentful awareness of an advantage enjoyed by another, paired with a longing to acquire that advantage
NOTE: the advantage can be a person, an object, or an intangible (popularity, lifestyle, etc.)

PHYSICAL SIGNALS:
Staring
Glowering
The mouth turning down
Lips parting slightly
A tightening under the eyes
A thinning mouth
Chin poking forward
Squinting
Baring the teeth slightly
A pouty bottom lip
Crossing the arms over the chest
Shoulders hunching slightly
Leaning closer
Reaching
Flaring nostrils
A coveting gaze that drifts to the symbol of envy (the advantage)
Being snarky or rude, seemingly without cause
Shoving one's hands into pockets
Twitching hands
Hands tightening into fists
Muscles bunching
Turning away from the advantage and stalking off
Swallowing frequently
Rubbing the hands over one's clothing
Feet and torso facing the advantage
Licking or sucking on the bottom lip
Sweaty hands
A reddening of the face
Rubbing at or massaging one's chest as if pained
Stroking or pinching one's throat
Taking a step toward the person or object one wants
Obsessive behavior (stalking, making a plan to acquire the advantage)

INTERNAL SENSATIONS:
Quick heartbeat
Ribs squeezing tight
Rising body temperature

A pulling sensation in the gut
Dry throat
Sucking in breath through clenched teeth

MENTAL RESPONSES:
A strong desire to touch, hold, and own
Anger at the unfairness or injustice
Unkind thoughts about the other person
Frustration
Scheming ways to acquire what another has
Self-loathing
Fantasizing about the advantage
An inability to commit to or focus on anything else
Dissatisfaction with what one does have
A feeling of entitlement: *I deserve it* or *That should be mine*

CUES OF ACUTE OR LONG-TERM ENVY:
Feeling that life isn't worth living without the advantage
Grabbing or stealing the coveted object
Fighting or arguing with the envied one to release frustration
Falsely belittling or minimizing the attributes of the desired advantage or object
Irrational thinking
Making demands: *Give it to me.*
MAY ESCALATE TO: DETERMINATION (54), RESENTMENT (130),
ANGER (22), DEPRESSION (48), JEALOUSY (102)

CUES OF SUPPRESSED ENVY:
Congratulating or offering praise
Forcing a smile
Acknowledging the object and complimenting it
Attempting not to stare
Watching from a distance

WRITER'S TIP: *When crafting the details of a fight scene, remember that less is more. Too many details create a play-by-play feel which can come across as mechanical.*

EXCITEMENT

DEFINITION: the state of being energized or stimulated and provoked to act

PHYSICAL SIGNALS:
A wide grin
Eyes that sparkle and gleam
Laughing
Bouncing from foot to foot
Squealing, hooting, yelling
Telling jokes
Chest bumping with others
A loud voice
Singing, humming, chanting
Slam-dunking trash into a barrel after a game or event
Babbling or talking over one another in a group setting
Fanning oneself
Pretending to faint
Verbalizing thoughts and feelings without hesitation
Lifting someone up or swinging them around
Trembling
Acting hyper, immature, or foolish out of a sense of fun
A ruddy complexion
Moving about, being unable to stay still
Good-natured shoving and pushing
Waving the arms, using grand gestures
Drumming one's feet against the floor
Hugging, grabbing onto someone's arm and holding it
Bumping shoulders
Raising up or bouncing on tiptoe
Phoning or texting to share news or pass on the excitement
Speed-talking with others, heads close together, gossipy
Throaty laughter
Getting the giggles
Friendly demands: *Tell me! Show me! Let's go!*
A body that's constantly in motion (nodding, bobbing, weaving, pacing)
A distinct walk, a fast-paced strut
Making eye contact with others, confidence
Displaying affection with friends or loved ones

INTERNAL SENSATIONS:
Lightness in the chest
A fast pulse
Dry mouth
Heightened senses

Breathlessness
Adrenaline rush

MENTAL RESPONSES:
Camaraderie with others
Imagining what could happen
Enjoyment of the communal energy
Impatience

CUES OF ACUTE OR LONG-TERM EXCITEMENT:
A need to run, jump, scream, whoop it up
An intense desire to share the feeling with others
A beaming face
Racing heartbeat
Sweating
A hoarse voice from screaming, yelling, or shouting
A loss of inhibitions
MAY ESCALATE TO: SATISFACTION (136), HAPPINESS (84), ELATION (68), DISAPPOINTMENT (56)

CUES OF SUPPRESSED EXCITEMENT:
Controlling one's movement with intent
Biting down on a smile
Swallowing a laugh or shout of glee
Feeling like one's insides are vibrating
Smoothing down clothing
Eyes that glow with inner light
Nodding rather than speaking

WRITER'S TIP: If you're stuck on how to show an emotion, form a strong image of the scene in your mind. Let the scene unfold, and watch the character to see how they move and behave.

FEAR

DEFINITION: to be afraid of; to expect threat or danger

PHYSICAL SIGNALS:
Face turning ashen, white, pallid
Hair lifting on the nape and arms
Body odor, cold sweats
Clammy hands
Trembling lips and chin
Tendons standing out in the neck, a visible pulse
Elbows pressing into the sides, making one's body as small as possible
Freezing, feeling rooted to the spot
Rapid blinking
Tight shoulders
Staring but not seeing, eyes shut or crying
Hands jammed into armpits or self-hugging
Breath bursting in and out
Leg muscles tightening, the body ready to run
Looking all around, especially behind
A shrill voice
Lowering the voice to a whisper
Keeping one's back to a wall or corner
Shaking uncontrollably
Gripping something, knuckles going white
Stiff walking, the knees locking
Beads of sweat on the lip or forehead
Grabbing onto someone
Eyes appearing damp and overly bright
Stuttering and mispronouncing words, tremors in the voice
Jerky movements, squirming
Licking the lips, gulping down water
Sprinting or running
Sweeping a hand across the forehead to get rid of sweat
Gasping and expelling one's breath as if pained
Uncontrollable whimpering
Pleading, talking to oneself
Flinching at noises

INTERNAL SENSATIONS:
An inability to speak
Shakiness in the limbs
Holding back a scream or cry
Heartbeat racing, nearly exploding
Dizziness, weakness in the legs and knees

A loosening of the bladder
Chest pain
Holding one's breath, gulping down breaths to stay quiet
A stomach that feels rock hard
Hyper-sensitivity to touch and sound
Adrenaline spikes

MENTAL REACTIONS:
Wanting to flee or hide
The sensation of things moving too quickly to process
Images of what-could-be flashing through the mind
Flawed reasoning
Jumping to a course of action without thinking things through
A skewed sense of time

CUES OF ACUTE OR LONG-TERM FEAR:
Uncontrollable trembling, fainting
Insomnia
Heart giving out
Panic attacks, phobias
Exhaustion
Depression
Substance abuse
Withdrawing from others
Tics (a repetitive grimace, a head twitch, talking to oneself)
Resistance to pain from rushing adrenaline
MAY ESCALATE TO: ANGER (22), TERROR (154), PARANOIA (114), DREAD (64)

CUES OF SUPPRESSED FEAR:
Keeping silent
Denying fear through diversion or topic change
Turning away from the cause of the fear
Attempting to keep one's voice light
A watery smile that's forced into place
Masking fear with a reactive emotion (anger or frustration)
False bravado
Over-indulgence in a habit (nail biting, lip biting, scratching the skin raw)
A joking tone, but the voice cracks

WRITER'S TIP: Prime readers for an emotional experience by describing the mood of a scene as your character enters it. If your character is antsy, the reader will be too.

FRUSTRATION

DEFINITION: vexation caused by unresolved problems or unmet needs; the feeling of being hindered

PHYSICAL SIGNALS:
Pinching the lips together
Holding hands behind the back, gripping one's own wrist
Rushed speech
Tapping one's fingers to release energy
Pointing with an index finger
Scratching or rubbing the back of the neck
Shaking the head
Jerky movements (talking with the hands, changing direction mid-stride)
Pacing in short spans
Stiff posture, rigid muscles
Clenching the jaw
Speaking through the teeth with forced restraint
An impatient snort or sneer, cursing under the breath
Drawing breath and releasing it before speaking
Splaying hands out wide to stretch, then relaxing them
Baring one's teeth
Throwing hands up in an "I give up" gesture
Stalking away from someone, leaving in a huff
Attempting to hurt through name-calling and personal jabs
Speaking without thought, often leading to regret
Slamming a door
Grabbing one's hair in clumps, looking up at the sky
A heavy sigh
Laying one's head down on the table
Stilted speaking
Eyes squinting, tightening
A harried appearance
Running hands through the hair
Fists tight, fingernails biting into the palms
A pinched, tension-filled expression
Scrubbing a hand over the face
Pounding a fist against the tabletop
Scrunching up the face and then releasing, trying to regain calm
Holding one's head in one's hands
A high chin
Arms crossing in front of the chest
Clumsiness due to rushing (slopping coffee, knocking something over)
Theatrical groaning
Restlessness

INTERNAL SENSATIONS:
Throat closing up
Hardening of the stomach
Tightness in the chest
High blood pressure
Headache
Jaw pain

MENTAL RESPONSES:
Extreme focus on problem solving
Replaying a scene or event over and over in one's mind, obsessing over it
Self-talking to calm down, to think straight
A need to ask questions and rehash information
Reining in one's emotions before damaging relationships

CUES OF ACUTE OR LONG-TERM FRUSTRATION:
Shouting, yelling, ranting, screaming, or criticizing
Crying, sobbing
Pleading or bargaining: *Please stop!*
Storming out of a room
An inability to sleep or relax
Profuse sweating
Using more force than necessary (stomping feet, throwing instead of handing off)
A display of violence (kicking, grabbing, shaking, or destroying something in release)
A tantrum (screaming, body flung down on the floor, crying)
MAY ESCALATE TO: CONTEMPT (38), ANGER (22), IMPATIENCE (94)

CUES OF SUPPRESSED FRUSTRATION:
Gritted teeth
Swiping at tears, trying to hide them
Silence or minimal responses
Briefly closing one's eyes
Taking a deep breath
Scraping a hand over the face as if to wash away emotion
Excusing oneself and leaving
Trying to shake or roll tension from the shoulders

WRITER'S TIP: *Use a character's intuition to draw the reader more fully into the scene. If you show what has primed their intuition clearly, the reader's own gut will respond and they will pay extra close attention. The flash of intuition must pay off in some way to complete the circle.*

GRATITUDE

DEFINITION: thankfulness; feeling grateful or appreciative

PHYSICAL SIGNALS:
Eyes that are soft, filled with an inner glow
Clasping another's hand or forearm
Tapping a loose fist against the heart
Placing a hand on the chest
Tearing up
Laying a hand on one's heart then gesturing to a person or group
Pressing fingers to smiling lips
Repeating one's thanks and appreciation
Holding onto someone's hand for longer than necessary
Hugging, showing affection
A light squeeze during a handshake
A smile that has a genuine build and lights up the face
Steady eye contact
Open palms
Saying *Thank you*
Moving closer, into another's personal space
Forming a steeple with hands and pressing them to lips
Offering praise for others
An emotion-rich voice
Offering small touches to connect
Laying a hand on someone's back or shoulder
Nodding, eyes glowing
Offering a gift, favor, or boon of appreciation
Raising one's palms to the sky and looking up
Complimenting
Clapping vigorously
Body and feet pointed forward
Offering a wave
A two-fingered salute
Tipping the head back for a moment and closing the eyes
Bowing or curtseying
Blowing a kiss
Offering a wave of thanks

INTERNAL SENSATIONS:
Tingling warmth in the limbs
A release of all bodily tension
A feeling of expansion in the chest
Heart that feels "full"
A comfortable warmth in the face

Weakness in the knees

MENTAL RESPONSES:
Desiring to repay another's kindness and support
Feeling overwhelmed in a good way
Wanting to drink in the moment, to remember this feeling forever

CUES OF ACUTE OR LONG-TERM GRATITUDE:
Worship
Falling to one's knees
A desire to do anything to repay
Joyful tears
A feeling of connection and love
MAY ESCALATE TO: SATISFACTION (136), PEACEFULNESS (116), HAPPINESS (84), ELATION (68)

CUES OF SUPPRESSED GRATITUDE:
Closing the eyes
Ducking the head to hide one's expression
Avoiding eye contact with others
Quick, darting glances to express a hidden thanks
Offering a distraction or changing the subject

WRITER'S TIP: *Make it a goal to offer the reader something unexpected in every scene, be it an emotional reaction, a roadblock to trip the character up, or a snippet of dialogue that sheds new light on the events unfolding.*

GUILT

DEFINITION: a feeling of culpability over an offense (either real or imagined)

PHYSICAL SIGNALS:
Averting or lowering one's gaze
Turning away
Shifting about
Chin dipping to the chest, adopting a slumped posture
Blushing
Reacting defensively
Short-temperedness
Consuming antacids
Repetitive swallowing
Lying
Sweating
Grimacing, lip biting
Avoiding a person or place
Talking too much or too fast
Keeping at a distance
Rubbing the nose or ears
Shoulders drawing up, elbows tucking into the sides
Closing or curling one's hands inward
Stuttering, growing flustered
Joking to lighten the mood or distract others from the truth
Seeking comfort by touching one's own hair, neck, or clothing
Pinning the arms against the stomach
Becoming unnaturally quiet or still
A quivering chin
Muttering tearfully to oneself
Anxious movements (pawing a hand through the hair, pacing)
A cracking voice
Pulling at one's collar
Taking a deep, pained breath and closing the eyes
Staring down at one's feet
Palms hidden (stuffed into pockets, held behind the back)
Darting glances at the person wronged
Following the one wronged, trying to convince oneself to confess
Inflicting pain on oneself as a penance
Destroying one's own possessions
An inability to join in fun activities or be with friends
Looking pale, having a harried or haunted look
Not showing up for work or school, letting grades slip

INTERNAL SENSATIONS:

Upset stomach
Tight chest
Pain in the back of the throat
Loss of appetite
Thickness in the throat

MENTAL RESPONSES:

Replaying what happened, anxiety
Thoughts filled with self-loathing
Wishing one could go back and change what happened
Desiring to confess or share the pain or burden with another
Brooding, retreating inward, withdrawing from others
Paranoia that others know and are passing judgment
An inability to concentrate on anything else

CUES OF ACUTE OR LONG-TERM GUILT:

A lack of interest in one's own appearance or wellness
Drinking until passing out (to forget), drug use
Insomnia
Depression
Exhaustion
Nightmares
Crying, sobbing, hitching breaths
Flight response—running away, unable to deal with the consequences
Growing reclusive, cutting oneself off from others
Self-mutilation
Self-loathing
Attempting suicide as a way out
MAY ESCALATE TO: CONFLICTED (34), REGRET (122), SHAME (140), REMORSE (128)

CUES OF SUPPRESSED GUILT:

Becoming excessively resourceful or helpful to make up for earlier failure
Fidgeting
Hiding one's mouth behind a hand
Changing the subject
Deflecting attention
Throat clearing
Verbally denying having anything to do with the event

WRITER'S TIP: Character bibles can help you keep track of hair, eye and clothing choices for each character, keeping the continuity from the first page to the last.

HAPPINESS

DEFINITION: a state of well-being or joyful contentment

PHYSICAL SIGNALS:
An upturned face
Smiling
Humming, whistling, singing
A relaxed appearance
Telling jokes, laughing frequently
Laugh lines
Raised, prominent cheekbones (from smiling)
Eyes that dance, sparkle, or shine
A bubbly or light voice
Rapid speaking
Buying gifts for others or offering tokens of kindness
Stretching out the legs, adopting a wide, open stance
Giving someone the thumbs-up
Sitting up, straight and alert
Fluid movements
Offering compliments
Swinging the arms while walking
Enthusiastic waving
A polite manner
Stepping lightly, skipping
Initiating physical contact with others
Infusing one's speech with positive words
Showing a talkative nature and courtesy with strangers
Spontaneity
Lightly rapping one's fingers (as if to internal music) on a leg or other surface
Swinging or tapping one's foot to an easy beat
Satisfied, catlike stretches
Expressing enjoyment of the senses (swaying to music, savoring food)
Nodding or leaning in, actively showing interest
Bouncing on the toes
Clasping hands to the chest
Offering encouragement and support
Quick movements, no hesitation
An overall visage that glows or radiates
Holding the arms out wide as if to hug the world
Initiating random acts of kindness

INTERNAL SENSATIONS:
A feeling of breathlessness
Heat that radiates through the chest

Tingling hands
Lightness in the limbs
A feeling of weightlessness

MENTAL RESPONSES:
Positive thinking
Desiring to spread joy and make others feel good
Noticing the small things (smelling the roses, so to speak)
Helpfulness
Being at ease with the world, content
Showing patience
A bright outlook (glass half full)
A desire to be with loved ones or friends
Fearlessness
Benign risk taking for fun

CUES OF ACUTE OR LONG-TERM HAPPINESS:
Joyful tears
Shaking with excitement
Big movements (leaping, fist pumping, running)
Happy bursts of screaming, shouting, laughter, squeals, giggles
Shows of affection
Spinning in a wild circle
Dancing
MAY ESCALATE TO: ELATION (68), GRATITUDE (80), SATISFACTION
(136), PEACEFULNESS (116)

CUES OF SUPPRESSED HAPPINESS:
Pressing the lips tight to keep from smiling
Difficulty staying still
Taking deep, calming breaths
Bouncing lightly in place
Averting the face
Fiddling with things to keep hands and feet from twitching
Carefully-masked features, but eyes that betray the true emotion
Putting away happy thoughts to savor later
Intense concentration on something or someone else
Hiding a joyous expression with one's hair
Holding a hand over the mouth to cover a smile
Pinching oneself and using the pain to help contain the emotion

WRITER'S TIP: *To increase tension in a scene, think about what is motivating your character, and which emotions could get in the way. Introduce an event that creates the very emotions the character wishes to avoid.*

HATRED

DEFINITION: to loathe or detest; to feel animosity toward

PHYSICAL SIGNALS:
Fists that shake
An intense, fevered stare
Clenched jaw, grinding teeth
Rigid and defined forearm muscles
Uttering dark, hurtful words meant to provoke
Stiff posture, square shoulders, a lurching walk
Shoving, pushing, tripping
Bearing the teeth
Fingers retracting, turning claw-like
Shouting, screaming, swearing
Lunging at an enemy
Spittle flying while yelling
A red face and neck
Sweating
Visible vein throb
A corded neck
Walking off, refusing to stay in another's presence
Switching shifts or altering a schedule to avoid an enemy
Tightness in the face, skin stretched into a snarl
An animalistic growl in the throat
Flaring nostrils
A grip that unintentionally crushes or breaks (snapping a pen, etc.)
A tense body, on the verge of springing
Bullying, cyber trolling
A mouth that curls with dislike, sneering
Spitting at someone or in their direction
Reaching out to throttle, hit, or cause pain
Shoving people aside to reach the enemy
Angry tears
Cursing, swearing
A scathing tone
A shaking voice
Using friends to help ostracize or bring the enemy low
Initiating hateful gossip, setting the enemy up, starting rumors
Wrenching an enemy's arm to stop them from leaving
Acting on violent urges (throwing a chair, destroying property)

INTERNAL SENSATIONS:
Loud breaths, a heaving chest
Pain in the jaw from clenching or grinding teeth

A pounding heartbeat
Headache
Rising body temperature
Strain or soreness from tense muscles
Roaring in the ears

MENTAL RESPONSES:
A dark mood that no one can reach through or dispel
Rash decisions, impaired judgment
Irrational thoughts, taking risks to get even
A desire to carry out a vendetta (via vandalism, theft, etc.)
Single-minded focus on how to destroy another
Humiliation fantasies featuring the enemy
Actively wishing for harm or misfortune to happen to another

CUES OF ACUTE OR LONG-TERM HATRED:
An inability to enjoy positive things or happiness
Difficulty eating and sleeping
Isolation
Fixating on an enemy, stalking
Deriving pleasure from violent fantasies involving an enemy
Committing crimes against the enemy
Assault or murder
MAY ESCALATE TO: PARANOIA (114), RAGE (120)

CUES OF SUPPRESSED HATRED:
Clamping the teeth shut to contain hard words
Taking deep breaths to calm oneself
Seeking out a distraction or diversion
Leaving the situation or presence of an enemy
Surrounding oneself with supportive friends

WRITER'S TIP: *One way to create emotional intensity is to have the character remember the stakes on the cusp of taking action. Worry over the outcome can add a slice of desperation to any scene and create a compelling emotional pull for the reader.*

HOPEFULNESS

DEFINITION: a bright, promising outlook; optimism

PHYSICAL SIGNALS:
Holding one's breath
Raising the eyebrows and offering a questioning gaze
Leaning in
Clutching at the chest or belly
Muttering *please* repeatedly under the breath
Clasping hands under the chin (in a prayer gesture)
A face that seems to shine
Gently biting the lip
Covering the mouth with a hand, eyes wide and shining
Deep breaths
Wiggling, squirming
Verbalizing the pros, not the cons
Strong eye contact
Smiling
Stiff posture, an air of readiness
Smoothing one's clothing to appear collected or worthy
Nodding along as another speaks
Holding still in expectation
Rapid swallowing and nodding
Chattiness, babbling
Lips parting slightly
Asking others to reaffirm the chances of success
Shifting back and forth
Making promises to convince others of one's worthiness
Offering commitment, to show one's ability to meet expectations
Attentiveness to tasks or people connected with one's goal
Restlessness
Licking the lip with cautious hope
Exhaling while the eyes look up
A gaze that darts to a symbol of hope (a friend in the know, a table of judges)

INTERNAL SENSATIONS:
A flutter in the belly
A light-hearted feeling
Tingling limbs
A jolt through the body
A floating sensation, like all one's burdens have been removed
Breath that temporarily bottles up in the chest

MENTAL RESPONSES:

A willingness to believe that everything will be all right
A strong awareness of one's surroundings
Thinking positive thoughts
A sense of calm
Focusing on improvement (studying, working extra hard)
Refusing to consider, speak of, or listen to negatives
Preparing for the best case scenario

CUES OF ACUTE OR LONG-TERM HOPEFULNESS:
Hands clasped in prayer, pressed to the lips, eyes closed
Quivering breaths
Shakiness
Tears
A trembling voice
Whimpering
MAY ESCALATE TO: EAGERNESS (66), EXCITEMENT (74),
DISAPPOINTMENT (56)

CUES OF SUPPRESSED HOPEFULNESS:
Locking hands together to force stillness
Mentally reducing high expectations
Reminding oneself of obstacles or competition
Pressing the palms downward to stave off over-confidence
Keeping one's face blank
Looking down or away

WRITER'S TIP: *Force your characters to make choices between bad and worse. Readers will empathize with your character, remembering their own past when they faced a similar dilemma.*

HUMILIATION

DEFINITION: feeling degraded or mortified, worthless or cheap

PHYSICAL SIGNALS:
Body collapsing in on itself
A bowed head
Shoulders curling over chest
Angling torso away from others
Uncontrollable shuddering or shivering
Hair hanging in face, hiding the eyes
A downward gaze
A flushed face
Hitching chest
Eyes dull, lifeless
Pulling down a shirt hem (covering gesture)
Body shielding (if holding onto an object)
Hands clutching at stomach
Covering face with hands
Bottom lip or chin trembling
Whimpering
Throat bobbing
Arms falling to sides, lifeless
Uncontrolled tears
Flinching at noise or from being touched
Huddling, crouching
Trying to cover body with hands
Neck bending forward
Movement is slow, jerky
Knees locked tight together
A loss of coordination
Cold sweat
Stumbling, staggering
Backing up against a wall, sliding into a corner, hiding
Visible tremors coursing through the body
Hands gripping elbows
Pigeon toes (tilted inward)
Sobs trapped in throat
Drawing knees up to the body's core
Wrapping arms around self
Runny nose

INTERNAL SENSATIONS:
Weakness in legs
Sluggish heartbeat

90

Pain in chest
Rapid swallowing
Dizziness, a sense of vertigo
Ribs squeezing
Body feels broken
Skin tightens (crawls)
Loose muscles
Hot eyes and cheeks
Nausea

MENTAL RESPONSES:
Self-loathing
Shattered thoughts
A feeling of nakedness, of being on display
A need to hide or flee that supersedes all else
Wanting it to end at all costs

CUES OF ACUTE OR LONG-TERM HUMILIATION:
Curling up on the floor
Hiding behind something, against something
Crying, blubbering, hitching sobs
Willingness to escape by any means
A desire to die, for the emotional pain to end
MAY ESCALATE TO: DEPRESSION (48), REGRET (122), SHAME (140), ANGER (22), HATRED (86)

CUES OF SUPPRESSED HUMILIATION:
Numbness in mind and body
Becoming passive and disengaged
Closing off all thoughts of what is happening
Not speaking or making any sound
Sending the mind "somewhere else"
A disconnect between the mind and body

WRITER'S TIP: Add conflicting emotions for a richer experience. A character might feel excitement and pride at purchasing their first car, yet worry that they might be extending themselves too far financially. This inner conflict helps to humanize a character to the reader.

HURT

DEFINITION: suffering grief or mental pain; feeling wounded or aggrieved

PHYSICAL SIGNALS:
Eyes widening, yet brows are furrowed
Swallowing hard
Lowering the head, the neck appearing to shrink
A slow, disbelieving head shake
A trembling chin
Mouth falling open
Flinching, starting
Color draining from the face
Saying *How could you?* as an accusation
Verbalizing betrayal in a strangled tone: *Leave me alone!*
Hunching over as if choking down a sob
Pressing a fist to the lips
Biting down on one's bottom lip
Gripping a fistful of shirt at the chest level
Holding a hand up, warding others off
Clutching the stomach
The body crumpling in on itself
A hitching chest
Drooping shoulders
Weakness in the knees
An uneven step
Displaying poor balance and coordination
A hand pressing against the throat or breastbone
Stuttering, choking out words
Letting out a whimper
Eyes that water
The mouth opening, but no words form
Sending someone a long, pained look and then breaking eye contact
A hanging head
Retracting the arms, bringing them close to the torso
Stumbling back a step
Backing up
Spinning away
A grimace that lingers
Clutching at oneself, elbows pressed to the sides

INTERNAL SENSATIONS
Dizziness
Stomach hardening, nausea
A painful tightness in one's throat

Constricting lungs, making it hard to breathe
Heartbeat seeming to slow or stop momentarily
Weakening muscles, trembling in the limbs
Spots flashing in one's vision

MENTAL RESPONSES:
The sense that time has stopped
Thoughts spinning, focusing inward
Shock, disbelief
Dredging up history, trying to understand how it led here
Feeling broken inside

CUES OF ACUTE OR LONG-TERM HURT:
A sense of betrayal that rocks the mind to the very core
A collapse in body posture
Tears, sobbing
Running away
Reacting with anger (screaming, slapping, hitting)
MAY ESCALATE TO: DEPRESSION (48), ANGUISH (24), ANGER (22)

CUES OF SUPPRESSED HURT:
Visible swallowing
Unnatural stiffness
Pinching the lips tight to keep them from trembling
Tensing the body to ward off shaking
Lifting the chin
Forcing oneself to maintain eye contact

WRITER'S TIP: *A natural way to describe a character's appearance is to show them interacting with their environment. A sense of movement also allows this type of description to flow with the scene as it progresses.*

IMPATIENCE

DEFINITION: feeling restless or short-tempered; having a desire for immediate change, relief, or gratification

PHYSICAL SIGNALS:
Raising one's eyebrows
Placing hands on the hips
Scowling
Head tilting back, gaze looking up
Crossing the arms
Standing or sitting stiffly
A tapping foot
Folding the hands
Pursing one's lips
Fiddling with cuffs or jewelry
Glancing repeatedly at the clock
Pacing
A hard jaw line, a jutting chin
Clicking one's fingernails against a table
Fidgeting instead of sitting or standing still
Narrowing eyes, having an intense focus
Interrupting, talking over someone else
Compressing the lips while someone else speaks
Being unnerved by annoying tics (loud breathing, pen clicking)
Frowning
A sharp tone
Massaging the temples, as if weary
Pinching the bridge of the nose and squeezing the eyes tight
Attention that snaps toward sound or movement
Door watching
Complaining under the breath: *Where is he?* or *This is taking too long!*
A clenched jaw, gritted teeth
Whining, grumbling, or pouting (small children)
Letting out a loud breath
Moving about (sitting then standing, choosing a different chair)
Toying with items (turning a cup, mangling a paperclip)
Muttering, shaking the head
Tilting the head to the ceiling and letting out a heavy sigh
Uncrossing and re-crossing the legs
Tension in the face, shoulders and neck
Using the body to nudge, push, or block (line jumpers)
Repeatedly running the hands through the hair
Veiled anger or light sarcasm

INTERNAL SENSATIONS:
Breathing that grows heavier, louder
Rising body temperature
Feeling exhausted or strained to the limits
Headaches

MENTAL RESPONSES:
Mentally berating a time-waster
Wishing time would speed up
Running through how to do something faster or more efficiently
Attention straying to other things
Asserting mental restraint to avoid snapping

CUES OF ACUTE OR LONG-TERM IMPATIENCE:
Slapping a hand against the table
Barking orders, yelling
Cutting people off
Taking over a project or duty
Telling the speaker to move on and get to the point
Redirecting the focus to allow things to proceed better
Setting a time limit
Making demands
Resorting to the physical (pushing, shoving)
MAY ESCALATE TO: IRRITATION (100), FRUSTRATION (78), ANGER
(22), SCORN (138)

CUES OF SUPPRESSED IMPATIENCE:
A frozen smile
Going for a walk
Using the time to run an errand or complete a task
Attempting to distract oneself in an effort to be patient
Rooting in a purse or pocket as a distraction
Checking and rechecking a phone for messages
Fussing with appearance (brushing away lint, checking fingernails)

> **WRITER'S TIP:** *Never let the reader notice the writing. Overusing metaphors, similes, descriptive terms, and repeated body language can pull the reader out of the story.*

INDIFFERENCE

DEFINITION: a state of apathy, casualness, or disinterest

PHYSICAL SIGNALS:
Shoulders are lowered and loose
A slow, steady gait
Arms hanging limply at the sides
Shrugging half-heartedly
Long pauses before responding
Staring blankly or emotionlessly
Lifting a hand loosely, palm up in a "Who cares?" gesture
Placing hands in one's pockets
Leaning back or away
Looking sleepy or glazed
Speaking in a flat voice
Smiling politely, not genuinely
The body sagging while seated, lacking tension
A wandering gaze
Picking at lint, scratching at cuticles, etc., to show that interest is lacking
Closing one's eyes to shut everything out
Texting during an event or while someone speaks
Not bothering to answer someone's questions
Being non-responsive during a group discussion or debate
Ignoring something being handed over (a file, business card, etc.)
Turning away
A nonchalant attitude
Speaking only when spoken to
Not responding to jokes or personal exchanges
Pointedly ignoring another person or situation that draws others in
Relaxed posture
An unhurried exit
Focusing on one's shoe, scuffing at the ground, etc., rather than giving due attention
Responding with *Whatever* or *So?*
Randomly changing the topic
Yawning
Mimicking boredom (slumping in one's seat, tapping a pencil)
Half-lidded eyes
Muttering *Uh-huh* or *Yeah* when it seems appropriate
Being easily distracted by other things (TV, a hot girl walking past)

INTERNAL SENSATIONS:
A lack of energy
Slow, even breaths

MENTAL RESPONSES:
Zoning or tuning others out to concentrate on other things
Wandering thoughts
A lack of empathy
Thinking about the time or future events

CUES OF ACUTE OR LONG-TERM INDIFFERENCE:
A disconnect with one's life or society
A fading sense of empathy
Falling into a routine
Meaningless interaction with others
Finding little day-to-day joy
Ignoring the pain or suffering of others
MAY ESCALATE TO: IRRITATION (100), ANNOYANCE (26),
CONTEMPT (38), RESIGNATION (132)

CUES OF SUPPRESSED INDIFFERENCE:
Smiling and pretending to pay attention
Nodding along as someone speaks but not actively listening
Asking a few token questions
Making an excuse to leave

WRITER'S TIP: To create a fluid, emotional arc in your story, make sure your character's feelings build in intensity and complexity as the novel progresses.

INSECURITY

DEFINITION: feeling unsure of oneself or displaying a lack of confidence

PHYSICAL SIGNALS:
Smoothing down clothing
A self-deprecating laugh
Breaking eye contact and shrugging
Keeping one's hands in pockets
Fidgeting
Checking one's breath
Throat clearing
Visible blushing
Speaking in a too-quiet voice
Licking or biting the bottom lip
Petting or stroking one's own hair (comfort gestures)
Covering up (pulling a jacket tighter, holding one's elbows)
Holding the knees and legs tightly together
Awkwardly mirroring the behavior of others
Choosing loose clothing over tight, revealing ones
Asking for reassurance from others
Brushing off compliments or putting oneself down
Looking down while walking
Staying at the edge of a group, seeking the corner of a busy room
Tucking the hands behind the elbows
Wrist twisting
Not smiling, or offering a smile that fades quickly
Visible tension in the muscles
Rubbing one's forearms
Needing advice or instruction on what to say or do
Laughing too loudly, or at odd times
Clutching an item to the chest (book, binder, purse)
Tapping the leg to settle nerves
Hiding behind one's hair
Biting nails or picking at loose threads on one's clothing
Staying at a distance
Holding a hand close to the face while speaking
Difficulty speaking or offering opinions
Rubbing at one's lips
Wearing too much makeup
Rushed speech, stammering
Increased sweat output during uncomfortable moments

INTERNAL SENSATIONS:
A heartbeat that races when one feels confronted

98

A roiling stomach
Uncontrollable flushes of heat
An uncomfortable, dry throat

MENTAL RESPONSES:
Difficulty making decisions
Over-thinking problems or choices
Obsessing over one's own flaws and shortcomings
Alert to others, to see how they react and what they do
Agreeing only to avoid a confrontation
Fixating on the talents and strengths of others
Comparing oneself to others and finding oneself lacking

CUES OF ACUTE OR LONG-TERM INSECURITY:
Holding onto a comfort item (a special piece of jewelry, a picture)
A bent spine
Blushing when noticed or spoken to
Avoiding social situations
Acting skittish around people
Panic symptoms when put on the spot
Preferring to do things alone
Wearing plain clothing to reinforce invisibility
Difficulty making friends
Choosing a seat in the back of the room or away from others
Seeking interaction online rather than in person
MAY ESCALATE TO: UNEASE (158), WARINESS (160), WORRY (162),
PARANOIA (114), EMBARRASSMENT (70)

CUES OF SUPPRESSED INSECURITY:
Tossing the hair
Thrusting the chest out
Standing taller, squaring one's shoulders
Forcing oneself to maintain eye contact
Deflecting questions or concern
Rushing into decisions to prove decisiveness
Mimicking others who display confidence
Risk taking
Lying
Inserting oneself into conversations

WRITER'S TIP: *Scenes do not happen in a vacuum. Don't forget to include setting, thoughts or verbal cues that allude to the passage of time.*

IRRITATION

DEFINITION: impatience and displeasure; the sense of being bothered

PHYSICAL SIGNALS:
The lips pressing together, pursing, or flattening
Face tightening
Narrowing eyes, squinting
Rubbing the back of the neck
Watching the source furtively
Frowning
Crossing one's arms
A glance that returns to the source of irritation
Pulling or plucking at clothing as if that is the source of discomfort
Fidgety movements (scraping the hair back, curling one's fingers)
Turning one's attention to someone else
Adopting a challenging tone, arguing
A hard smile
Poking a tongue lightly into the cheek and inhaling a long breath
Asking pointed questions
Changing the subject
Forcing a laugh
Raising the voice
Opening the mouth to say something, then thinking better of it
Biting the inside of the cheek
Restless legs (crossing and uncrossing, unable to stand still)
Going silent, disengaging from conversation
Feigning interest in other things to buy time and regain control
Making small, jittery movements with the fingers
Breathing through the nose (audibly to others)
Curling one's toes
Clasping the hands tightly, a whitening of the knuckles
Interrupting
Repeating a mannerism (scratching an eyebrow, adjusting glasses)
Spots of color entering the cheeks
Clenching one's teeth

INTERNAL SENSATIONS:
Tightness in the chest
Tense muscles
Sensitive skin
Quickened pulse
A twitchy feeling in the extremities
Raised body temperature
Tightness in the jaw and facial muscles, causing discomfort

MENTAL RESPONSES:
Dismissing the source as unworthy
Trying to put the upsetting information out of one's mind
A desire to talk the situation over with someone else
Wishing someone would stop or shut up
Stubbornly sticking to one's belief even if it doesn't make sense
Clouded judgment
Judging others and their performance or contribution

CUES OF ACUTE OR LONG-TERM IRRITATION:
Openly challenging another's logic or standpoint
Swearing
Negative language: *You don't know what you're talking about!*
Sarcasm
Name-calling
Facial tics
Rising blood pressure
MAY ESCALATE TO: FRUSTRATION (78), ANGER (22)

CUES OF SUPPRESSED IRRITATION:
Avoiding the source
Two-faced behavior
Nitpicking
Passive-aggressive comments
Forcing oneself to not look at or acknowledge the source
Leaving the room or situation to clear thoughts
Seeking to discredit the source so as not to have to believe him or her

> **WRITER'S TIP:** *Make body language unique to the character. Do they lift themselves up in their shoes as they wait in line? Do they run a finger along the seam line of their jeans when deep in thought? Creative emotional mannerisms help characters leap off the page.*

JEALOUSY

DEFINITION: hostility toward a rival or one suspected of enjoying an advantage
NOTE: the advantage can be a person, an object, or an intangible (love, success, etc.)

PHYSICAL SIGNALS:
Adopting a sullen look
Making a slight growl or noise in the throat
Bitterness at watching how others respond to the rival
Quick, sharp movements (swiping tears from cheeks, shoving hair out of eyes)
Pursing or pressing lips flat
Crossing arms in front of chest
Clenching teeth
Muttering unkind things under breath
Starting rumors, acting catty
Picking on someone weaker for a sense of power and control
Sneering
Ugly laughter
Shouting insults, name-calling
Taking a step closer, fists clenched
A visible flush in cheeks
A pinched expression
Tight muscles
Body mimicking that of the rival
Trying to "one-up"
Issuing a challenge to the rival that contains an element of risk
Criticism
Spitting in the direction of the rival
Swearing
Kicking at nearby objects
Showing off
Pulling stunts or pranks to regain attention
Rudeness, saying something that is a "low blow"
Reckless behavior
Gloating when the rival falters or shows weakness

INTERNAL SENSATIONS:
Burning sensation in the chest or stomach
Stomach hardening
Breaths coming coarser, faster
Spots or flashes in vision
Pain in jaw from clenching teeth

MENTAL RESPONSES:
A desire to vent and voice the rival's unworthiness to others
Rash decision-making (quitting a team, storming out of a party)
A flash of anger when the rival is mentioned
A desire to discredit, or take away the rival's power
Wishing harm
A desire for revenge
Turmoil at having negative feelings
Focusing solely on the rival's negative attributes
Comparing oneself to the rival in the eyes of peers
Rejecting the advantage (choosing to pursue another girl instead)

CUES OF ACUTE OR LONG-TERM JEALOUSY:
Jeering, running someone down, bullying
Picking fights
Unhealthy obsession with the rival
Indulging in petty crime (keying the rival's car, etc.)
Engaging in self-mutilation as a release
Negativity spilling into other parts of one's life
Self-doubt, a lack of confidence
A relationship categorized by negativity, passive-aggression, and criticism
Feeling fake from wearing two faces for so long
Dishonesty with self and others
A pattern of subversively trying to undermine the rival in the eyes of others
MAY ESCALATE TO: ENVY (72), DETERMINATION (54), ANGER (22),
HATRED (86)

CUES OF SUPPRESSED JEALOUSY:
Acting normal to the rival's face but talking negatively behind their back
Watching the rival furtively, privately
Striving to also excel at whatever is desired
Grouping with others who also lack whatever is desired
Kissing up to gain approval through association
Trying not to focus on the rival
Telling oneself that it doesn't matter
Attempting to think positive thoughts about the rival

> **WRITER'S TIP:** *In each scene, think about the lighting. Full sunlight, muddy clouds washing everything in grey, the onset of sunset or even darkness...light and shadow can affect a character's mood, amp their stress level or even work against their goals.*

LONELINESS

DEFINITION: the feeling of being isolated or cut off

PHYSICAL SIGNALS:
A longing gaze
Disinterest in one's appearance (bland clothing, lackluster hair)
Slumped shoulders, limp posture
A monotone voice
Looking down when walking in public
Watching people furtively
An expressionless, unsmiling face
Sullenness
Being generous to others in order to curry favor
Spying or eavesdropping on others to feel a part of something
Filling schedule with work or volunteering to avoid downtime
Using books, the internet, and TV to escape
An expression that crumples at other peoples' affection displays
Hugging oneself
A lack of eye contact
False bravado
Tears, sadness
A heavy sigh
Talking to oneself
Feeling a sense of comfort from a full mailbox (even junk mail)
Stroking self (rubbing an arm absently for contact)
Using bright or eccentric clothing choices in an attempt to get attention
Doting on someone or something (a neighbor, a pet)
Talking to strangers to feel connected
Relishing opportunities to talk or engage (mail deliveries, etc.)
Rambling when conversing with others
Adhering to a routine (eating the same meals, visiting the same park)
Living vicariously through an alter ego or avatar (social networking, gaming)

INTERNAL SENSATIONS:
A thickness in the throat, signaling the onset of tears
A longing so intense it manifests itself as an ache or pain
Insomnia
Fatigue

MENTAL RESPONSES:
Avoiding crowds, large events, or social situations
A desire to be included, wanted
Anger, bitterness
Daydreaming about people one would like to have relationships with

A feeling of unworthiness

CUES OF ACUTE OR LONG-TERM LONELINESS:
Doubting oneself, a lack of confidence
Weight gain
Believing that one is unattractive or has a boring personality
Uncontrollable crying bouts
Despairing of ever being able to change
High blood pressure
Workaholic tendencies
Bingeing to compensate (eating, drinking, shopping, gambling)
Hoarding pets
Suicidal thoughts
MAY ESCALATE TO: SADNESS (134), HURT (92), DEPRESSION (48), RESIGNATION (132)

CUES OF SUPPRESSED LONELINESS:
Committing too quickly to anyone who shows interest
Choosing negative relationships over being alone
Being too friendly and coming across as desperate
Frequently calling family or friends
Solitary activities that show a craving for contact (people watching from the porch)

WRITER'S TIP: Body movements should never be random. Everything a character does should have a specific intent: to achieve an end, reveal emotion, or to characterize.

LOVE

DEFINITION: deep affection, attachment, or devotion for another

PHYSICAL SIGNALS:

Moving to get closer or touch
Smiling at nothing
A beaming expression, glowing cheeks
Strong eye contact, very little blinking
Focusing on the other's best attributes
Taking large, deep, savoring breaths
A yearning look
Licking one's lips
Unconsciously parting the lips
A light, bouncing step
A silly grin, laughing, talking non stop
Leaning against one another
Lying in the other's lap
Using pet names or terms of endearment
Mooning over photos or representations of a love interest
Listening to and connecting with love songs
Adopting a silly love-struck tone when communicating
Nervous behaviors (fiddling with the hands, moistening one's lips)
Flirtatious talk or saying: *I love you*
Torso and feet pointing toward the loved one
Playful shoving and grabbing
Sharing secrets and desires
Affectionate touches (arm stroking, holding hands, kissing, hugging)
Sitting together so the legs touch
Putting an arm around someone's shoulders
Realigning hobbies or interests to match the other's
Hooking a hand in the other person's belt or pocket
Ignoring or neglecting other friends to be with the significant other
Writing notes or poetry to the other person
Offering gifts of time, value, or thoughtfulness
Talking to friends about the special person, asking for advice
Obsessively checking the phone to see if the love interest has called
Constant texting back and forth
Doodling hearts and names
Dieting or working out in an effort to improve one's appearance
Watching romantic movies

INTERNAL SENSATIONS:

A fluttering in the stomach, a feeling of emptiness
A racing pulse

The heart beating, banging, or hammering
A hyper-awareness of the body
Weak knees or legs
A tingling or electrical jolt at accidental touches
Getting tongue-tangled

MENTAL RESPONSES:
Euphoria, pleasure at touching and closeness
Appreciating the world and everything in it
Losing track of time when with the other person
Mental fuzziness, distraction, daydreaming
Losing awareness of surroundings when love interest is near
Seeking ways to make a loved one proud
Worrying when too much time has passed without contact
A feeling of possessiveness, jealousy
Feeing safe and whole when together

CUES OF ACUTE OR LONG-TERM LOVE:
Exchanging personal effects (clothing, jewelry, keys)
Embracing the love interest's friends as one's own
Sharing finances and possessions
Enduring hardship to be with the love interest or make them happy
Putting the other's needs and desires first
Intimacy
Sharing hopes and dreams, becoming emotionally vulnerable
Future planning that centers around the love interest
Living together, a committed relationship, marriage
MAY ESCALATE TO: PEACEFULNESS (116), SATISFACTION (136),
DESIRE (50), ADORATION (14)

CUES OF SUPPRESSED LOVE:
Flushed skin
A high-pitched voice
Nervous laughter or giggling
Standing close yet not touching
Darting glances
Watching from a safe distance
An increased interest in the other person's personal life
Forcibly declaring that nothing's going on: *We're just friends*
An overall brightening when the other person enters the room

WRITER'S TIP: *Sentence structure is especially important when describing.*
Varied sentence length keeps the pace moving and livens up sensory detail,
avoiding a "dry report" feel.

NERVOUSNESS

DEFINITION: the state of feeling unsettled and being easily agitated

PHYSICAL SIGNALS:
Short, jerky movements
Pacing
Rapid blinking
Rubbing the back of the neck
Unbuttoning the top button of a shirt
Scratching or rubbing skin
Biting at lips
Jumpiness
Flighty hand movements, fidgeting
Clumsiness
Rubbing hands down one's pant legs
A lack of eye contact
Scraping a hand through the hair
Quick breaths
Crossing and uncrossing arms or legs
Eyeing the exits
Bouncing a knee (while sitting)
Repeated gestures (tie straightening, touching an ear)
Increased sweat, particularly on the hands
Tingling fingers and toes
Pupils appear dilated
Biting or picking at one's fingernails
Shaking out the hands
Clearing the throat
Facial tics
Stuttering, stumbling over one's words
Quick, high-pitched laughter
Restlessness (sitting, then standing)
Laughter that goes on for longer than normal
Closing the eyes and taking a calming breath
Rapid speaking, babbling
A change in the pitch, tone, or volume of the voice
Tackling a task to distract (cleaning, waxing the car)

INTERNAL SENSATIONS:
Acute senses
Nausea
Sensitive skin
Faintness
An empty feeling in the pit of the stomach

108

Quivering, twitchy muscles
A rolling or fluttery feeling (butterflies) in the stomach
Loss of appetite
Dry mouth
Heart palpitations
Headache

MENTAL RESPONSES:
The desire to flee
Erratic thought processes, irrational fears
Overreacting to noise
The mind going to the worst-case scenario
Wishing time would speed up

CUES OF ACUTE OR LONG-TERM NERVOUSNESS:
Vomiting
Fatigue or insomnia
Panic attacks
Withdrawal
Irritability
Ulcers and other digestive disorders
Weight loss or gain
Negative thought patterns
Indulging in alcohol, drugs, or chain smoking to take the edge off
MAY ESCALATE TO: INSECURITY (98), ANXIETY (30), FEAR (76), DREAD (64)

CUES OF SUPPRESSED NERVOUSNESS:
A pasted-on smile
Flexing the fingers, curling and uncurling
Clasping one's hands together
An unnatural stillness
Eyes that blink too much or don't blink enough
Not meeting anyone's gaze
Changing the topic
Avoiding conversation

WRITER'S TIP: *Body movement and external reactions alone will not create an emotional experience for the reader. Pairing action with a light use of internal sensations and/or thoughts creates a deeper emotional pull.*

NOSTALGIA

DEFINITION: the yearning for a return to a past period or situation

PHYSICAL SIGNALS:
An unfocused gaze
A slight smile
Slowly flipping through old pictures, stroking the pages
A relaxed posture
Eyes that fill with tears
Using a quiet voice
Cocking one's head to the side
Subdued laughter
A shallow sigh
An unhurried walk
Rubbing a hand against the heart
Slouching on a sofa, watching old movies
Slow, languid movements
Growing animated when memory is triggered (an old song on the radio, etc.)
Eyes brightening as memories are recalled
Keeping mementos from the happy time
Telling and retelling stories about the past
Seeking out those who shared the event
Gently touching memorable items (a baby blanket, wedding invitations)
Closing one's eyes to more clearly recall the memories
Trying to recreate a past event (burning the same scented candle, wearing the old clothes)
Seeing similarities in the present: *You look just like him* or *This is the same color as our first car*
Increased tenderness (sitting close, a quick kiss) for those who shared in the event

INTERNAL SENSATIONS:
Eyes prickling with tears
An excited flutter in the belly
An overall relaxation of the body
Breathing slows as a memory takes over
Dulled awareness (sitting in an uncomfortable position without feeling it)
Experiencing (to a lesser degree) the same physical sensations felt during the past event

MENTAL RESPONSES:
Losing track of the time while remembering
A desire to go back and visit the past
Mentally replaying past events

Satisfaction at having experienced the event despite any pain or loss resulting from it

CUES OF ACUTE OR LONG-TERM NOSTALGIA:
Discontentment with the way things presently are
Expressing more emotion about the past than the present
Spending large periods of time in the past
Hoarding tendencies
Neglecting current duties or relationships
An inability to move on
Depression
MAY ESCALATE TO: SADNESS (134), DEPRESSION (48), HAPPINESS (84)

CUES OF SUPPRESSED NOSTALGIA:
An austere lack of mementos from the past
Sniffing back tears
Rejecting opportunities to revisit the past (reunions, trips to the old house or hometown)
Not engaging in conversations about the past
Masking nostalgia with practicality: *I kept his toys so he could give them to his kids*

WRITER'S TIP: *When introducing and describing characters, parcel out personal details in small bits. Anything that isn't pivotal to plot or characterization can be left to the reader's imagination.*

OVERWHELMED

DEFINITION: to be overpowered or overcome by feelings or circumstances

PHYSICAL SIGNALS:
Bringing a shaky hand to the forehead
Holding a palm up to stop someone from dumping on more worry
Waving people away
Shoulders that drop or curl
A chest that caves in
Clutching at one's arms or stomach
Touching a temple while closing the eyes
A voice choked with tears
A chest that hitches
A quaking voice
Poor balance
Mumbling, muttering
Letting out an uncontrollable cry, sob, or whimper
Uncertain (almost drunken) steps
Sagging into a chair, leaning against a door frame or wall
Pulling the knees up to the chest, circling one's knees with the arms
Falling against another person
Shaking all over
Teary eyes
Difficulty forming responses
Holing up in a corner, placing one's back against the wall
Dropping or spilling things
Shaking the head repeatedly
A glassy stare, a glazed look
Staring down at one's empty palms
Crumpling to the floor
Putting one's hands over one's ears
Rocking back and forth
Closing the eyes
Inappropriate responses (laughing, screaming)
Leaning over with the hands on the knees
Hyperventilating
Loosening belts, collars, and other confining clothing
Touching one's fingertips to one's lips

INTERNAL SENSATIONS:
Weakness in the legs, a sudden need to sit down
A wave of heat or cold
Light-headedness
Difficulty breathing

An inability to eat
Noise sensitivity
Ringing ears
Tunnel vision

MENTAL RESPONSES:
Mental numbness
Retreating inward
Becoming non-responsive to others, almost catatonic
Wishing for comfort
The desire to be alone
An inability to focus
Indecisiveness

CUES OF BEING OVERWHELMED LONG TERM:
Flight
Snapping under pressure (screaming, yelling, hitting others)
Fainting or swooning
Weeping
Hysteria
Headaches
Hypertension
Muscle fatigue and soreness
Seeking comfort in unhealthy ways
Heart attack or stroke
Chronic fatigue, insomnia
Decaying physical health, hospitalization
MAY ESCALATE TO: ANXIETY (30), DEPRESSION (48)

SUPPRESSED CUES OF BEING OVERWHELMED:
Verbal denial: *I'm fine, really*
False smiles and confidence
Agreeability or false enthusiasm
Masking weakness with excuses: *Sorry, I stood up too fast*
Feigning a headache or other malady rather than admit one's limits

---

WRITER'S TIP: *When delivering emotional description, it's easy to rely too much on facial expressions. Instead, look down and describe what the arms, hands, legs, and feet are doing.*

PARANOIA

DEFINITION: excessive or illogical suspicion and/or distrust of others

PHYSICAL SIGNALS:
Startling easily
Clenching the jaw
Darting eye movements, a wide-eyed look
Excessive safety precautions (extra locks, guard dogs, video surveillance)
Fidgety hands that won't settle
Restless sleep, tossing and turning, insomnia
Backing away with raised hands
Flinching
Eyes that don't seem to blink often enough
Crossing the arms tightly over the chest
Muttering under one's breath, talking to oneself
Scratching compulsively
Sweating
Bloodshot eyes
Scouting for exits when entering a room
A heightened need for personal distance
Dependency on caffeinated beverages or drugs to stay alert
Pallid skin from lack of sunlight
A rumpled appearance
Accusing innocent people of planning or carrying out mischief
Facial tics, muscles that jump
A quick, erratic pace
Always looking over the shoulder or around the next corner
Weight loss
Plucking at clothing as if it chafes
Aligning with fringe groups and conspiracy theorists
Espousing far-out beliefs and opinions
Becoming easily offended
Jumping to the defensive
Verbally attacking any perceived opponents
Spouting inane or irrational arguments
Citing unreliable sources
Stubbornly adhering to one's beliefs no matter how outlandish
Perfectionist tendencies
Compulsive behaviors
Refusing food or drink prepared by others

INTERNAL SENSATIONS:
Heightened senses
Fatigue

114

Muscles that are always tense, ready to fight or run
Sensitivity to touch and sound
A racing heartbeat
Raw nerves and skin
High adrenaline level, jumpiness

MENTAL RESPONSES:
Seeing danger symbols in everything
Judging too quickly
A heightened sense of self-importance
Irrational responses, jumping to illogical conclusions
Mental fatigue from not getting enough sleep
Seeing and hearing things that aren't there
An inability to connect with others due to a lack of trust
Always seeing the worst-case scenario
Negative thought patterns
Feeling watched or followed
The belief that everyone else is deluded
Adhering to superstitious beliefs to stay safe

CUES OF ACUTE OR LONG-TERM PARANOIA:
Contacting the authorities for help against suspected assailants
An inability to maintain long-term relationships
Isolation
Living off the grid
The belief that one is no longer required to live by the laws of society
A complete break with reality, hallucinations
Rage
Anxiety attacks, phobias, psychosis
MAY ESCALATE TO: FEAR (76), ANGER (22), RAGE (120), HATRED (86), DESPERATION (52)

CUES OF SUPPRESSED PARANOIA:
Avoidance of social situations
Attempting to engage socially, but with wary and darting eyes
Agreeing with everything in an attempt to seem "part of the group"
Watching others and mimicking them as a way of appearing normal
A smile that is frozen, manic
A high voice or odd laugh
Using medicine or seeking therapy

WRITER'S TIP: *In dialogue, it's not always what a character says that's important, it's how they say it. (And sometimes it's what they are trying hard not to say!)*

PEACEFULNESS

DEFINITION: a state of calm that is devoid of strife, agitation, or commotion

PHYSICAL SIGNALS:
A relaxed posture
Smiling, grinning
Fingers loosely clasped in one's lap
Closed eyes, the head tipped back
Softened features that imply calm
Nodding to others in greeting
Leaning back, an arm hooked over the back of a chair
Taking a deep, satisfied breath
Using a friend's shoulder as a shelf for your elbow
An unforced laugh
Whistling or humming
Sparkling eyes, a weightless gaze
Enjoying an event (a movie, a concert in the park, a picnic)
Lying on the grass to soak up the sun
Catlike stretches
A warm voice, caring tone
Half-closed eyes, a lidded look of satisfaction
Lacing fingers behind the head
A wide stance, open demeanor
Languid movements
Rolling the neck back and forth
Looping the thumbs in the front pockets while standing
An easy walk, unhurried
A wandering gaze, taking in random things
A satisfied sigh
Unhurried speech
Contentedly taking more time to complete tasks
Expressing a greater interest in the happiness of others
Engaging in meaningful conversations

INTERNAL SENSATIONS:
Slow and easy breaths
Slack muscles
Loose limbs
Drowsiness
A lack of tension and stress that almost equates to a feeling of nothingness
A steady, calm pulse and heartbeat

MENTAL RESPONSES:
Being with others with no need to fill the silence

116

Satisfaction with the world at large
A feeling of connection to life
Having no desire to be anywhere else
Enjoying listening to others
Living in the moment, not acknowledging the past or future
Avoiding topics of conversation that will kill the mood
Delighting in even mundane, everyday tasks
A desire for everyone to experience such peace

CUES OF ACUTE OR LONG-TERM PEACEFULNESS:
A lessened need for worldly goods
Choosing to spend time with positive or like-minded people
A growing interest in spiritual or religious philosophy
A desire to maintain a positive status quo
Changing one's lifestyle to accommodate new beliefs (recycling, moving to the country)
Impatience with corporate greed and capitalism
A desire for more natural living
An increased awareness of one's body and what goes into it
Engaging in new and satisfying hobbies and interests
MAY ESCALATE TO: HAPPINESS (84), SATISFACTION (136)

CUES OF SUPPRESSED PEACEFULNESS:
Claiming that one's calm demeanor is simply tiredness
Forcing oneself to maintain a slight stiffness in posture
Pretending to disengage because of boredom

WRITER'S TIP: *Choose verbs carefully. The meaning of a sentence can be altered through the words used to describe action. Readers will see a character who trudges up the stairs as being in a different emotional state than one that bounds up them, two at a time.*

PRIDE

DEFINITION: proper self-respect arising from a significant achievement, possession of an item, or involvement in a relationship

PHYSICAL SIGNALS:
A high chin
Shoulders back
Chest thrust out
Standing tall with good posture, legs spread wide
A gleam in one's eye
A knowing grin
Perfectionism
Watching others to see their reactions
Verbalizing the ups and downs that led to this point
Calling friends and loved ones to tell them about an accomplishment
Direct or intense eye contact
A booming laugh
Becoming talkative
Lifting the heels and rising up slightly to emphasize words
Steering or dominating the conversation
Becoming extra animated when there's an audience
A grin that conveys secret knowledge
Thrusting oneself into the middle of an event or debate
A satisfied smile
Hooking thumbs into one's belt loops, thrusting the pelvis forward
Pulling in a deep breath
False modesty
Ignoring or overlooking any flaws associated with the pride item
A preoccupation with one's appearance
Standing with hands tucked in one's armpits, thumbs visible and pointing up
Running the hands through the hair, flipping hair back
Assuming a pose that's sexy or draws attention to one's best attributes
Appearing unaffected by what others think
Speaking first, thinking second

INTERNAL SENSATIONS:
The feeling of being taller, bigger, stronger
Lungs expanded to their fullest through deep, satisfied breaths

MENTAL RESPONSES:
Positive self thoughts
Preoccupation with one's achievements or successes
A feeling of being able to conquer the world
Wanting to be surrounded by supportive loved ones

A desire to share achievements with others
A tendency to judge people according to one's personal measuring stick
Over-estimating one's capabilities
Underestimating others
A sense of entitlement
Planning and seeking advantages

CUES OF ACUTE OR LONG-TERM PRIDE:
Enjoyment at proving others wrong
Bragging, obsessively talking about an achievement or material object
Praising group accomplishments as a way to remind people of one's own involvement
Reacting with anger or jealousy if one's reputation is impugned
Making radical statements or promises about future goals
Revisiting the source or place of accomplishment to feel empowered
MAY ESCALATE TO: SMUGNESS (144), CONTEMPT (38), CONFIDENCE (32)

CUES OF SUPPRESSED PRIDE:
Waving off a compliment
Passing the credit to someone else
Turning attention away from oneself
Seeking others' opinions as a form of validation

WRITER'S TIP: Understand your character's emotional range. For one character, intense situations may make them hyperventilate. For another, it might cause them to shift slightly while seated. Knowing how expressive a character is will help you find the perfect body cue to convey an emotional meaning.

RAGE

DEFINITION: violent and uncontrolled anger

PHYSICAL SIGNALS:
Flushed or mottled skin
Shaking extremities
Hands that clench and unclench
Wide eyes, showing the whites
Spittle building up in the corners of the mouth
Biting criticism and belittlement
Jabbing a finger in someone's face
A corded neck
Nostrils flaring
Lips pulling back, baring the teeth
Cracking the neck from side to side for intimidation
Muscles and veins straining against skin
A guttural roar
Planting the feet wide apart
Sudden explosions over seemingly little things
Pushing and shoving
Limbering up shoulders and neck as if readying to fight
Squeezing someone's arm to the point of bruising
Using insults to pick a fight
Cracking one's knuckles to intimidate
Pulling out a weapon (knife)
Finding something close to hand to use as a weapon (branch, rock)
Moving slowly and deliberately toward another person to intimidate
Barreling toward someone, uttering a scream or war cry
Fighting with no thought for one's own safety
Throwing or kicking things
Jumping to extreme anger with little provocation
Screaming
Threatening violence
Uttering death threats: *I'll kill you!*
Staring someone down to frighten them
Getting into someone's personal space
Manipulation

INTERNAL SENSATIONS:
A pounding in the ears
Increased blood flow to the extremities
Elevated pulse
Clouded vision
A dry throat from rushed breathing

Pain that is suspended until later
Adrenaline rushing through the body
A sensation of increased strength
An edgy, twitchy feeling
Tunnel vision or flashes in vision

MENTAL RESPONSES:
Being driven by the belief that one has been mistreated or done wrong
A desire for vengeance
Looking for a fight
Wanting to hurt someone, to see blood
A sense of release when violence is expressed
Not thinking or caring about consequences
A need to dominate or control
Difficulty focusing or concentrating

CUES OF ACUTE OR LONG-TERM RAGE:
Beating someone senseless
Committing assault or murder
Seeking out opportunities to react violently
Self-destructive addictions
Depression
Heart disease, stroke
Ulcers
An inability to cope with smaller problems over time
Insomnia
Fatigue
Destroying property
MAY ESCALATE TO: PARANOIA (114), REGRET (122)

CUES OF SUPPRESSED RAGE:
Unnatural silence
Uncontrollable body tremors
Punching a wall or object instead of a person
Clenched, grinding teeth
Pain in the jaw from clenched teeth
A tight smile that doesn't reach the eyes
Grabbing onto something secure (like a steering wheel) and shaking it violently
Punching or ripping apart something soft
Aggressive workouts

> **WRITER'S TIP:** *As your character reacts emotionally to circumstances within the environment, don't underestimate the importance of sensory details. Do textures bother them because of a heightened state? What sounds do they pick up on that they might not otherwise notice?*

REGRET

DEFINITION: sorrow aroused by circumstances beyond one's ability to control or repair

PHYSICAL SIGNALS:
Scrubbing a hand over the face
Laying a hand against the breastbone
A heavy sigh
A downturned mouth
Bent posture
Heavy arms, the shoulders pulled low
Apologizing
Trying to reason or explain
Eyebrows gathering in
A pained expression
Hands falling to the sides
Staring down at one's feet
Covering the face with the hands
Squeezing one's eyes shut
Lifting hands up and then letting them fall
Pinching the bridge of the nose, eyes closed
Wincing or grimacing
Rubbing the chest as if pained
Avoiding the victims (shame)
Seeking reconciliation (determination to set right)
Berating oneself for actions or choices
Losing the thread of conversations
Hiding behind one's hair
Shaking the head
A voice that loses its power
Using broken sentences or trailing off while speaking
Making a *tsking* noise or murmuring regret: *What a shame*
Asking questions about the fallout: *How did she take the news?*
Scrambling to reverse what was said or done
Increasing one's distance from others
Trying to fade into the background at social events
Putting oneself down

INTERNAL SENSATIONS:
A knotted belly
Insomnia
An inability to fill lungs completely
A nervous stomach
Loss of appetite

Dullness in the chest, a feeling of heaviness

MENTAL RESPONSES:
Self-loathing
The feeling that one deserves pain or judgment
Obsession with the person or event associated with the regret
Reliving past events
Thoughts that turn inward
Trying to forget the event
A desire to go unnoticed
Distractedness
Wishing it hadn't happened

CUES OF ACUTE OR LONG-TERM REGRET:
Not taking physical care of oneself
Weight loss
Withdrawing from society
Dropping out of clubs and groups
No longer finding joy in hobbies or favorite pastimes
Overcompensation in other relationships
Crying, sobbing
Self-destructive behaviors
Drug and alcohol abuse
Unsafe sexual practices
Abusive relationships
A string of broken relationships
Ulcers
A lack of intimacy with others
An inability to forgive oneself
MAY ESCALATE TO: SHAME (140), FRUSTRATION (78), DEPRESSION (48)

CUES OF SUPPRESSED REGRET:
Desperately seeking out new relationships
Talking about one's accomplishments as a way of winning people over
Making life-altering decisions (career change, a move, etc.) as a way to start over
Acting like the life of the party
Putting on a happy face

> **WRITER'S TIP:** *Watch for possible description crutches. Is the color "green" used too much? Does a sensory sound (like wind rustling through the trees) happen in multiple scenes? Keep track of these details to avoid overuse.*

RELIEF

DEFINITION: the alleviation or lightening of oppressive stressors

PHYSICAL SIGNALS:
Covering the mouth with a hand
Shaking head and closing the eyes
Gasping
Trembling hands
Reaching out to another for comfort
Slumping posture
A slow smile
Using humor to lighten the moment
Shaky laughter
Sagging against a wall or person
Pressing the palms to the eyes
Asking for the good news to be repeated
Wobbly legs
Buckling knees
Stumbling back a step
Flopping back in a chair
A gaping mouth
Struggling to speak, to find the right words
An unsteady walk
Crying or calling out in release
Asking redundant questions to assure that the moment is real
Eyes going up, looking heavenward
Letting out a huge breath
Rocking back and forth
Eyes shining, locked on the source of relief
A slight moan
Lips parting
Showing kinship with others involved (hugging, reaching for their hands)
Pressing one's hands to the stomach
A palm pressed to the heart
A bowed head
Starting to fall then catching oneself
Closed eyes, compulsive nodding
Letting the head fall back
Uttering a soft curse or thanking God
Making the sign of the cross (if religious)

INTERNAL SENSATIONS:
Dry mouth
Weak muscles

An unexpected release of all tension
Tears welling up behind eyelids
A sudden lightness or giddiness

MENTAL RESPONSES:
Wanting to be held
A desire to be still and let the relief sink in
Gratitude
Jumbled thoughts
An inability to formulate an appropriate verbal response
Postponement of residual loss or pain until a later time

CUES OF ACUTE OR LONG-TERM RELIEF:
Breaking down, tears
Exuberant responses (jumping up and down, shouting, running, hysterical crying)
Collapsing
An expanding feeling in the chest
Light-headedness
A thick throat
MAY ESCALATE TO: HAPPINESS (84), EXCITEMENT (74), GRATITUDE (80)

CUES OF SUPPRESSED RELIEF:
A deliberately quiet exhale
Briefly closing the eyes
Drawing a deep breath through the nose
Biting the lips to keep from smiling
Swallowing and nodding
Narrowed eyes, when it's necessary to focus on something besides the source of relief
Not thinking about it, putting it off to savor later
Inattentiveness

WRITER'S TIP: *When a character is hiding an emotion, the cues are not as noticeable. In this circumstance, it's often more effective to show the emotion through change—altering a speech pattern, falling back on habits, posture shifts, etc.*

RELUCTANCE

DEFINITION: unwillingness; aversion

PHYSICAL SIGNALS:
Stalling gestures (taking time to think, turning away)
A hard, obvious swallow
Wetting the lips
Tense arms, shoulders, or face
Hesitant steps
The head pulling back as the shoulders push forward
Responding slowly (accepting an item, offering assistance)
Pressing lips together
Glancing around uneasily
Hands that shake, nervous twitching
Hands almost curling into fists and then straightening
A grimace or pained look
Eyebrows squeezing together
Stuttering, stammering
Making excuses
Lying
Tentatively reaching out or touching
Holding a hand up, warding someone or something off
Suggesting someone else to help or act instead
Shaking the head
A hand fluttering to the lips or neck
Nervous habits (running hands through the hair, pacing, repetitive gestures)
A too-quick smile
Glancing at one's watch
Jumpiness
Moving toward an exit
Putting distance between oneself and the requester
Biting the lip or nails
Pinching the bridge of the nose and tightly squeezing the eyes
Changing the topic or diverting attention
Closed body language (hands up, crossed arms)
Leaning or turning away from the person making the request
Asking for time to make the decision
Expressing skepticism
Asking questions for clarification
Not meeting the requester's eyes
Not engaging in further conversation
Answering with a "maybe" response
Muttering negatives: *No* or *I don't want to*

INTERNAL SENSATIONS:
Taking a deep breath before acting
A tightening chest
Slight tenseness in the muscles
A heaviness in the stomach

MENTAL RESPONSES:
A desire to get away from the person making the request
Indecision
A mind that is clearly distracted
Guilt
Searching for ways to get out of whatever is requested
An inability to focus on anything but the decision to be made
A need to justify one's reluctance

CUES OF ACUTE OR LONG-TERM RELUCTANCE:
Resentment
A tight or roiling stomach
Avoidance of the source
A strained relationship
MAY ESCALATE TO: SKEPTICISM (142), DEFENSIVENESS (44), ANGER (22), FEAR (76), DISGUST (60), RESENTMENT (130), DREAD (64)

CUES OF SUPPRESSED RELUCTANCE:
Agreeing, then not following through
Hints about being busy or overly stressed
A rising antipathy toward the person responsible for the situation
Passive-aggressive comments
Deflecting, acting as if the request is absurd
Joking comments to deflect
Revealing true feelings to a third party, hoping they'll pass the information along

---

WRITER'S TIP: *Avoid brand dropping to characterize. Brand names come and go, and can date your writing. Instead use other clues to convey your character's personality, strengths or shortcomings.*

REMORSE

DEFINITION: distress resulting from guilt over wrongdoing; a desire to undo or fix

PHYSICAL SIGNALS:
Heartfelt apologies
Asking to talk
Following the aggrieved party
Repeatedly returning to the scene where past events took place
Head down as the eyes look up
Watering eyes
A hand that cups the mouth
Holding one's head in hands
Tears that one does not try to hide or control
Silence
Offering restitution
Using the victim's name in dialogue when they are present
Telling the unvarnished truth
Speaking without hesitation when answering
A quivering chin
Holding the stomach
Shoulders that curl over the chest
Not defending oneself against attack (verbal or physical)
Crumpled body posture
Staring down at the floor
Clasping the hands together in the lap
Shaking
Begging for forgiveness
Shoulders that quake with repressed sobs
A pleading tone
A pale or unhealthy complexion
Dark circles under the eyes
Hollowed cheeks
Reaching out to touch and then pulling back as if not worthy
Readily agreeing to a punishment or pronouncement
A voice that cracks
Verbalizing responsibility for what happened
Quiet answers to questions
Arms hanging at the sides
Still hands and feet
Obedience
Breaking into sobs

INTERNAL SENSATIONS:
A stomach that feels hard
Runny nose
Nausea
Gritty or dry eyes from lack of sleep
A lump in the throat

MENTAL RESPONSES:
Mentally berating oneself over an action or poor decision
Wanting to face the consequences
Obsessing over finding a way to repay the debt
Empathy for the other party and what they are going through
Being honest about one's role in the situation
Relief for owning up to wrongdoing

CUES OF ACUTE OR LONG-TERM REMORSE:
Weight loss
Headaches
Heart problems
Self-destructive behaviors out of the belief that one does not deserve happiness
Desperation to balance the scales or resolve the situation
A complete life change (taking up charity work, finding God, etc.)
MAY ESCALATE TO: SHAME (140), REGRET (122), DETERMINATION (54)

CUES OF SUPPRESSED REMORSE:
Avoiding friends who are also culpable (if a group act)
Lying about feelings
Claiming that the victim was partly responsible
Making an excuse to leave
Dropping out of activities, school, or work on false pretenses
Moving away

WRITER'S TIP: *Description is clearest when a writer adheres to the real order of events in a scene. Show the action (stimulus), then the reaction (response) and a reader will clearly see how A leads to B.*

RESENTMENT

DEFINITION: indignation toward an act, remark, or person; feeling injured or insulted

PHYSICAL SIGNALS:
A pinched mouth
Arms crossed over the chest
A flat look, narrowed eyes
Scowling
Increasing one's personal distance from others
Complaining
Rudeness
Pouting (children)
Catty behavior
Name-calling
A voice that rises in volume or intensity
Arguing
Looking past someone rather than at them
A hard expression
Arms straight, hands locked into fists
Refusing to be bought off through kindness or thoughtfulness
Shunning the source
A stiff stance
Purposely ignoring someone's conciliatory efforts
Muttering under the breath or cursing
Twisting the mouth, a soured expression
Belittling another's status or accomplishment
Tension in the neck and shoulders
Pointing and jabbing the air for emphasis
A curling lip, showing the teeth
A sharp, defined jaw line
A tart tone, snapping at others
Sabotaging another's projects or actions out of a sense of being wronged
Talking behind someone's back, gossiping
An unkind smile
Shaking the head in disapproval but not saying anything
Balling the hands into fists
Walking out of the room
Spinning away in a huff, stomping up the stairs
Shutting a door with more force than necessary

INTERNAL SENSATIONS:
Tension headaches
Pain in the jaw

A tight chest
Constricting the throat
High blood pressure
Stomach troubles or ulcers

MENTAL RESPONSES:
Unkind thoughts toward the target
Frustration at unfairness or a lack of justice
Fantasizing harm or the downfall of another
Moodiness
Wanting to be alone
Fixating on a person or situation to the detriment of other relationships
A desire to bring others in and create a mob mentality of resentment

CUES OF ACUTE OR LONG-TERM RESENTMENT:
Weight gain
Illness
Insomnia
Arriving late, calling in sick, or refusing work shifts to avoid the source of
resentment
High blood pressure
Seeking revenge
MAY ESCALATE TO: ANGER (22), HATRED (86), JEALOUSY (102)

CUES OF SUPPRESSED RESENTMENT:
Walking away
Keeping silent
Changing the topic to something safe
Putting on a smile

WRITER'S TIP: *When exposing the reader to a new scene, person, or object, it can be useful to have some description or opinion delivered through a secondary character's dialogue. What they notice and how they respond provides an opportunity to characterize.*

RESIGNATION

DEFINITION: the state of surrendering, often with little or no resistance

PHYSICAL SIGNALS:
Sighing dejectedly
Slumped shoulders
Blank features
Stooped posture
Shuffling footsteps
Small steps
Tears
A monotone voice
Becoming less verbal over time
Dull eyes
A chin that trembles
Answering with a small nod
Sagging facial features
Limp hands and arms
Unwashed hair
Wrinkled, disheveled clothes
A loss of appetite
Disinterest in former hobbies or passions
Making oneself small (hugging oneself, squatting down, fetal position)
Avoiding eye contact
Being at a loss for words
Lethargically giving comfort to others (rubbing their back, patting their shoulder)
A shake of the head
Head tipping back on the neck to look skyward
Agreeing, but without emotion
Clasping the hands together
Leaning forward, elbows on knees
Staring off at nothing
A hanging head
Loose jaw
A half-hearted shrug
A long exhale
Muttering, mumbling
Holding the head in the hands
Propping a cheek on a fist
Unresponsive or slowed reactions to stimulus
Grunting, one-word answers
Purposely closing the eyes, as if to process
Excessive sleeping

INTERNAL SENSATIONS:
A falling or dropping sensation
Emptiness, numbness
A lack of emotion
Weakness in the muscles

MENTAL RESPONSES:
A determination to make the best of the situation (glass half-full)
An inability to focus or concentrate
Feeling directionless
Confusion: *How did this happen?* or *What will happen to me now?*
The sense that nothing will ever be the same
Feeling powerless over the present or future
Believing that one has failed

CUES OF ACUTE OR LONG-TERM RESIGNATION:
Depression
Retreating inward
Disconnecting from others
Doubting oneself, a decrease in confidence
Apathy
Becoming submissive, giving up control
MAY ESCALATE TO: SADNESS (134), DISAPPOINTMENT (56), DEFEAT (42)

CUES OF SUPPRESSED RESIGNATION:
Whining, questioning, offering token weak arguments
Squaring shoulders, but without any real force or strength
Offering a small display of anger
Acting like giving in was a choice, not the only option

WRITER'S TIP: *Too many emotional internalizations in a scene can slow the pace considerably. If the thoughts are key, try shifting some of these to active, realistic dialogue. It will increase the pace and still reveal the character's feelings.*

SADNESS

DEFINITION: characterized by grief or unhappiness

PHYSICAL SIGNALS:
Puffy face or eyes
Eyes appear red
Running makeup
Splotchy skin
Sniffing, wiping at nose
Wincing
Drooping shoulders, a bowed spine
Voice is tearful or breaks
Staring down at one's hands
Stooped posture
Rubbing the heel of a palm against chest
Decreased coordination and clumsiness
A distant or empty stare
A flat, monotone voice
Downturned facial features
Covering the hands with the face
Arms hang at the sides, slack
Rubbing or pressing a fist against the chest
Crossing one's arms, holding onto one's shoulders
Slumping rather than sitting straight
A heavy-footed walk
A slack expression, wet, dull eyes
Bending forward, laying head on arms
Movements that lack energy
A trembling chin
Crying
Digging for tissues
Touching a cross or fingering jewelry for comfort
Drawing the limbs close to the body
Staring down at one's empty hands
Clutching a token that is the focal point for the emotion
Quaking shoulders
Decreased interaction with the world at large

INTERNAL SENSATIONS:
An aching chest
Hot or gummy eyelids
A scratchy throat
A runny nose
Soreness in the throat and lungs

134

The world spinning or seeming to slow down
Heaviness or tightness in the chest and limbs
A heart that is breaking or aching
Blurred vision
Lack of energy
Body feels cold

MENTAL RESPONSES:
Difficulty responding to questions
An inability to see where the future might go
Turning inward, withdrawing
A desire to escape the sadness (through sleep, drink, companionship)
A need to be alone
Wishing comfort from others
Avoiding the painful subject, denial
Wanting the pain to end

CUES OF ACUTE OR LONG-TERM SADNESS:
A pained keening
Tears pouring, dripping, or coursing
Hyperventilating, shortness of breath
Loss of appetite
Despair, hopelessness
Despondency
MAY ESCALATE TO: NOSTALGIA (110), DEPRESSION (48),
LONELINESS (104)

CUES OF SUPPRESSED SADNESS:
Turning away
Halting one's speech to gain control
Deep breaths or gulping at the air
Biting the lip
Blinking
Changing the subject
Sipping a drink or taking a bite to eat (to prove to others one is stable)
Quivery smiles
Hands gripping each other or an object
Covering or cupping the mouth with one's hand
Focusing on alleviating another's pain rather than one's own
Excusing oneself to use the restroom or get a drink to be alone

WRITER'S TIP: *In dialogue, be on the lookout for where your character "thinks" instead of "responds" verbally. This leads to unnatural, one-sided conversations.*

SATISFACTION

DEFINITION: the state of being content or fulfilled

PHYSICAL SIGNALS:
A high chin and exposed neck
A crisp nod
Smoothing the front of a shirt or tugging down the sleeves
Offering a "thumbs-up"
Giving a toast or praise
Clapping someone on the back
A wide stance, fists on hips, elbows wide
Surveying the finished product with a pleased expression
A raised eyebrow and a *See?* look
A sleek walk that draws the eye (catlike, deliberate)
A shy, confident, radiant, or cocky smile
Apt dialogue that sums up the situation perfectly
Saying *I told you so!*
A puffed-out chest
Shoulders back, straight posture
A fist pump
Clapping
Fingers forming a steeple
Including others in the moment
Bragging
A hand casually anchored on the hip
Stretching the arms out wide
Leaning back, at ease and in control
A deep, gratifying sigh
Whistling or humming
A distant, unfocused smile
Taking deep breaths, savoring the moment
Unhurried, relaxed movements
A direct manner (eye contact, strength in voice)
Rewarding oneself

INTERNAL SENSATIONS:
A hyper-awareness of others and their reactions
A lightness in the chest
Warmth spreading through the body
A tiredness that is fulfilling rather than exhausting

MENTAL RESPONSES:
Happiness over a job well done
Euphoria, exhilaration

Contentment
Gratification
Increased confidence
Looking forward to a well-earned rest
Mentally fixating on the recent success
Not paying attention to one's surroundings
Self-congratulations
Generosity to others as a result of feeling gratified
A desire to tell everyone about the success

CUES OF ACUTE OR LONG-TERM SATISFACTION:
Justified possessiveness
An expression of supreme confidence, a glow
Cockiness
MAY ESCALATE TO: HAPPINESS (84), SMUGNESS (144), PRIDE (118), GRATITUDE (80)

CUES OF SUPPRESSED SATISFACTION:
Twitching lips
Hiding a smile behind a hand
Bouncing lightly on the toes
Getting away at the first opportunity to tell someone the good news
Settling back in a chair in release

WRITER'S TIP: Loners and their lack of social interaction present specific writing challenges. To break up long stretches of introspection, maintain some character relationships. Remember that a person can be lonely even when surrounded by people; use the dialogue, dysfunction, and drama that go along with those relationships to keep the pace moving forward.

SCORN

DEFINITION: extreme contempt or derision; regarding as inferior

PHYSICAL SIGNALS:
A biting remark
Belittling comments that remind the target who has the upper hand
A smirk
A quick, disgusted snort
Looming over the target
Crossed arms, a wide stance
Sarcasm
A tight jaw
A harsh squint
A deliberate eyebrow raise and head tilt
Pulling down glasses and looking over the rims with a flat gaze
Flapping a hand in dismissal
Bullying tactics
An exaggerated eye roll or upward glance
Blowing out a breath that rattles the lips
Insulting the target in front of others
A thrust-out chest
An ugly twist to the mouth
Encouraging others to speak up against the target
Limited verbal responses, as if the target isn't even worth talking to
Laughter at another's expense
A wrinkled nose
Flicking a hand in front of one's nose as if to get rid of a bad smell
A tight mouth, as if tasting something bad
Narrowed eyes
Staring the target down
Applauding in a deliberately false fashion
Projecting hurtful observations: *I'd be embarrassed if I were you!*
Anger at being touched or addressed by the target
Calling attention to another's weaknesses
Ignoring the target
Speaking slowly to emphasize hurtful words
Leaving to show that the target is not worth one's time
Apologizing to others for having their time wasted by the target

INTERNAL SENSATIONS:
A puffed-up feeling
Adrenaline rush at taking away another's power
Body temperature rises

MENTAL RESPONSES:

Elation at delivering a blow to an opponent through dialogue or action
Anger
A desire to put the person in their place
Superiority
Arrogance

CUES OF ACUTE OR LONG-TERM SCORN:

Asking questions to further incriminate the target
Egging the target on
Picking fights
Forcing the target into circumstances where he is sure to fail
Gathering other like-minded people and encouraging their scorn
Seeking to hurt through a "low blow" comment
MAY ESCALATE TO: ANGER (22), HATRED (86), ELATION (68)

CUES OF SUPPRESSED SCORN:

A blank, emotionless face
Becoming unresponsive to questions or action
Turning away
Shaking the head
A slight muscle jump in the cheek
Tightened jaw
Clamping one's lips tight to keep from saying anything
Making an excuse to leave

> **WRITER'S TIP:** *When describing a character's emotional state, pay attention to their voice. Does it rise or drop in pitch? Get louder or softer? Grow rough or silky smooth? Changes in pitch and tone are great indicators for when a character is trying to hide their feelings from others.*

SHAME

DEFINITION: the feeling that arises from a dishonorable or improper act; disgrace

PHYSICAL SIGNALS:
Cheeks that burn
Crumpling onto a chair or sofa
Pulling arms and legs in toward the core
Muttering *What have I done?* or *How could I let this happen?*
Using the hair to hide the face
Pulling a ball cap low
Pressing hands against one's cheeks
Dropping the chin to the chest
Wet eyes
A blank look
An inability to meet another's eyes
Crumpling under scrutiny
Shaking, trembling, shivering
Hunched shoulders
A perpetual slouch
Tears
A closed-off stance (crossing the arms, making oneself small, averting the head)
Pressing a palm over the lips to hold back a cry
Shaking the head
Letting out an uncontrolled moan
Punching fists against thighs to release frustration
Lashing out at others to transfer anger or blame
Arms hanging at the sides
Hitching breaths
A trembling chin
Shielding the body, angling away from those bearing witness to shame
Pulling and tugging at one's clothes as if they can make one less visible
Vandalism of one's own things
Loss of interest in one's personal appearance
Seeking out second chances (fawning, begging, following others) to regain self worth
Lying or doing whatever it takes to keep a shameful secret

INTERNAL SENSATIONS:
Hypersensitivity to noise, crowds, activity
Flu-like symptoms (nausea, sweats, tingling in chest)
Weak knees
Thickness in throat
Heat and tingling in face

Body tremors

MENTAL RESPONSES:
Flight reaction
Pulling away from friends and loved ones
Avoiding familiar places and activities
Self-loathing, berating oneself, anger, disgust
Risk-taking behaviors, hoping something will happen to balance the scale
Denial
An utter lack of self-confidence
A desire to fade into the background and avoid notice

CUES OF ACUTE OR LONG-TERM SHAME:
Self-violence (scratching, cutting, pulling hair)
Depression
Substance abuse
Eating disorders
Increased sexual activity
Panic attacks
Anxiety disorders
Perfectionist tendencies to balance the source of shame
Seeking power as a means of self-validation
Denial, diversion of blame to others
Suicide
Abusive relationships
Attempting to change one's appearance
The belief that one deserves pain
Rejecting help out of a desire to do penance
MAY ESCALATE TO: DEPRESSION (48), HUMILIATION (90), REMORSE (128)

CUES OF SUPPRESSED SHAME:
Shame is, by and large, private. People are always trying to hide this emotion so all cues for shame are naturally suppressed.

WRITER'S TIP: There are dozens of physical, internal, and mental responses to use when conveying a given emotion. Filter possible cues through what you know about your character. "Would my character react this way?" is a great question to ask to stay on the right track.

SKEPTICISM

DEFINITION: having a disposition of doubt or incredulity

PHYSICAL SIGNALS:
Pursing the lips in thought
Tilting the head and pausing
Shaking the head
Pressing the lips into a fine line
Raising the eyebrows
Clearing the throat
Fiddling with jewelry or other items
Shrugging
Nodding, but with a tight expression to show one is not fully committed
A confrontational stance
A smirk or eye roll
A hand flap that dismisses the person or their idea
Demanding proof or evidence to support
Listing the possible consequences
Polite verbal opposition
A condescending smile
Muttering negatives: *I don't think* so or *No way that would work*
Restlessness (pacing, tapping fingers, clock-watching)
A tightness in the face
Rigid body posture
Rubbing the back of the neck without making eye contact
Narrowed eyes
Biting or chewing on one's lip
Gossiping with others, running a person down for their choices or ideas
Sniping remarks
Licking one's lips
Hemming and hawing
Referencing similar events from the past that did not pan out
Bringing up everything that could go wrong
A purposeful shiver or shudder
Biting the fingernails
A heavy sigh
Walking away
Tapping a finger against the tabletop in an effort to drive a point home
Asking *Are you sure?* or *What if?* questions
A jutting chin
A silent look
Wrinkling the nose like there's a bad smell
A quick exhale through the nose, a snort

INTERNAL SENSATIONS:
Tightness in the chest
Increased heartbeat and pulse
Tense muscles
A flare of adrenaline, firing the brain to act

MENTAL RESPONSES:
Negative thoughts
Uncertainty
Honing in on flaws, either of logic or of a physical nature
A desire to change the speaker's mind or standpoint
Wanting to be around people with the same opinions

CUES OF ACUTE OR LONG-TERM SKEPTICISM:
Anger
Frustration
Passive skepticism becoming more overt
Looking for ways to discredit the speaker
A desire to shut the speaker up
The mind racing through possible arguments
Disbelief, that others can't see the truth
Actively seeking to bring people over to one's way of thinking
Becoming argumentative
MAY ESCALATE TO: UNCERTAINTY (156), SUSPICION (150), RESIGNATION (132), SCORN (138)

CUES OF SUPPRESSED SKEPTICISM:
Attempting to keep a neutral facial expression
Footsteps that drag
A quick widening of the eyes before schooling one's expression
Apologizing for not showing immediate support
Sitting still, hands clasped, mimicking interest and attention
Acting noncommittal: *Interesting idea*, or *That's something to think about*
Asking for a person to review the pros and cons again for clarity
Suggesting a trial basis as a solution
Requesting more time to reflect
A suggestion that perhaps more thought or study is needed

WRITER'S TIP: Don't make it easy for your heroes. Pile on the difficulties. Overwhelm them. Make it seemingly impossible for them to succeed so that when they do overcome, the reader will be properly impressed.

SMUGNESS

DEFINITION: supreme confidence in and satisfaction with oneself

PHYSICAL SIGNALS:
A jutting chin
Crossed arms
A thrust-out chest
Deliberately raised eyebrows
Cocking or tilting the head
A smirk or sneer
Direct, probing eye contact
Squinting and a hard smile
A dismissive nod or glance
Rolling the eyes
Aggressive teasing intended to put another in their place
A sigh conveying annoyance (a huff)
Waving a hand in dismissal
Leaning in aggressively as if to challenge
Rocking back on heels
Mean-spirited talk behind another's back
Projecting the voice, reinforcing who has the upper hand
Sarcasm: *Whatever*, or *Sure you are*, or *If you say so!*
A look that radiates superiority
Perfect posture, shoulders back, exposed neck
A determined walk, strut, or swagger
A loud voice, bragging, full of bluster
Using boisterous movements to draw attention to oneself
A wide stance
Criticism and belittlement
Talking over people, controlling conversations
Looking down one's nose at others
Dominant behavior (invading another's personal space, standing while others sit)
Lavishing praise on favored ones (children, friends, people in power)
An arrogant laugh
Preening (fussing with clothing, checking oneself in the mirror)
Flashy or dramatic clothing
Tossing one's hair back, a shake of the head
Adopting a pondering pose (hand clasping the chin as if struck by deep thoughts)
Settling back in a chair with exaggerated casualness
Movements that draw attention (waving a cigar, gesturing with a glass of wine)
A deliberate crossing of the legs or clasping of the hands
Fidgeting with jewelry in order to draw attention to it
Clapping someone on the back, overplaying closeness or friendship
Name-dropping

Rubbing it in with an *I-told-you-so*

INTERNAL SENSATIONS:
Warmth radiating throughout the body
A puffed-up feeling
Tingling in the chest
Heart rate rising due to adrenaline rush

MENTAL RESPONSES:
A firm belief in one's own rightness and superiority
Disdain for those who are unworthy
Over-confidence
A desire to belittle the unworthy and exalt one's own accomplishments
Gratitude at having risen above the rest
The belief that those who have not succeeded are to blame for their failure

CUES OF ACUTE OR LONG-TERM SMUGNESS:
Extreme pride in appearance and possessions
Careful consideration of friendships, purchases, places where one is seen
Reminding someone of a past mistake to rub it in
Choosing to spend time in environments that are a reminder of success
Generosity that displays power (hosting charity functions, etc.)
Acting as if rules do not apply or one is above the law
MAY ESCALATE TO: CONTEMPT (38), SCORN (138)

CUES OF SUPPRESSED SMUGNESS:
Making token acknowledgements to those who played a part in an outcome
Citing that luck was involved, but not meaning it
Preachy advice: *Do what I did and you'll succeed too.*

WRITER'S TIP: *When describing a character's feelings, the word "felt" is often a cue for telling emotion, not showing. Run a search for this word and challenge yourself on its use.*

SOMBERNESS

DEFINITION: having a dark or gloomy manner

PHYSICAL SIGNALS:
An unmoving stance
A voice devoid of emotion, deadpan
A grave expression
A sad or serious demeanor
Hands folded in one's lap
Sitting quietly
Flaccid yet unwelcoming (closed) body language
A tendency to look down
A thoughtful expression
Hesitation before speaking, as if weighing words
Dark or heavy observations
A bleak mood that affects others, lessens energy, brings people down
An inward gaze or unfocused stare
Loose posture
Speaking at the air rather than make eye contact with others
Hands clasped loosely behind the back and gaze down
A slow walk
Features are smooth, expressionless
Keeping arms and legs in close to the body
Movements are functional and precise
Unsmiling, humorless
Words are chosen deliberately
Not reacting to stimuli (laughter, excitement, activities)
Drab, colorless clothing choices
A grim twist to the mouth
Sedate mannerisms, minimal or economical movement
Eyes that look dark or serious
An unnatural stillness
A pensive expression
Food and drink lacks taste or does not bring enjoyment

INTERNAL SENSATIONS:
Fatigue, lacking energy
Heaviness in the limbs or muscles
A weighed-down feeling
Breathing is slow and even

MENTAL RESPONSES:
Subdued personality
A negative outlook

A desire to be alone
Difficulty engaging in conversation
Searching internally for answers rather than asking others

CUES OF ACUTE OR LONG-TERM SOMBERNESS:
Accepting a negative outcome or realization
Uninterested in hobbies or entertainments
Melancholy, gloominess
Shunning other people who are not of like mind
Inability to focus on the needs of others (children, family)
Apathetic toward goals, desires or upcoming events
MAY ESCALATE TO: DEPRESSION (48), RESIGNATION (132)

CUES OF SUPPRESSED SOMBERNESS:
Forced laughter
A too-frequent smile
Smiles that quickly fade
Agreeing to attend happy social events, then not showing
Smiles that don't reach the eyes
Light words delivered in a serious tone
Adding an adornment (a pin, fancy hat, a bright scarf) solely for appearances

WRITER'S TIP: If your scene includes a small dip into the past to retrieve information that has direct bearing on the current action, make sure there is an emotional component. Emotions are triggers to memory and help tie the present to the past.

SURPRISE/SHOCK

DEFINITION: unexpectedly struck with a feeling of wonder, joy, or fear
NOTE: can be negative or positive

PHYSICAL SIGNALS:
The mouth falling open
A hand flying to the chest
Fingers touching parted lips
A gasp
An incredulous stare or dazed look
Jerking the head back
Slapping hands against the cheeks
A playful swat at a friend for causing the surprise
Shuffling back a step or two
A yelp, gasp or squeal
A sudden stiffening posture, rigid muscles
Stopping mid-stride or stumbling
Hugging friends close by
Giddiness
Widening or bulging eyes, a double take
Shaking the head, voicing denial
Stuttering, stammering
A rise in vocal pitch
Grabbing onto a friend's arm
Hiding the face
Squeezing the eyes shut
Gripping the sides of the head as if to cover the ears
Spreading the fingers out in a fan against the breastbone
Touching the throat
Turning away (negative surprise)
Pulling books or packages tightly against one's chest
Raising a hand to ward off others from approaching or speaking
A shaky, soft, halting, or disbelieving voice
Asking simple questions for clarification: *Who? When? Why?*
A tentative smile that builds as surprise sinks in
A bark of laughter
Breaths that catch or hitch
Tipping or turning the head to the side

INTERNAL SENSATIONS:
Tingling skin
A heavy feeling in the stomach
Racing heartbeat
Breathlessness

A sudden coldness that hits at the core (if surprise is negative)
Disorientation, dizziness, or euphoria
A fluttery feeling in the belly
A flush of adrenaline tingling through the body

MENTAL RESPONSES:
Wanting to hide
Fuzzy thoughts, an inability to think
Embarrassment

CUES OF ACUTE SURPRISE (SHOCK):
Ducking, covering one's head with the arms
Collapsing from a perceived fright
Breathlessness
Tears or shakiness
Ducking the chin to hide the neck
Jerkiness in the legs, leaping back
Hands rushing toward the mouth to cover
Gasping or letting out a sharp scream
Clutching at one's chest on reflex
Muscles tightening, head drawing back stiffly
Flight reaction (running away, hiding)
Fight reaction (shoving the initiator, delivering a punch to release anxiety)
Arms drawing back to the body core in a protective flinch
Stuttering or speechlessness
Swearing or shouting
MAY ESCALATE TO: AMAZEMENT (18), HAPPINESS (84), FEAR (76), ANGER (22), RELIEF (124), DISAPPOINTMENT (56)

CUES OF SUPPRESSED SURPRISE:
One's smile going stiff in an effort not to lose it (negative)
Rapid blinking
Widening eyes
Lifting the eyebrows
A closed-lipped smile
Nodding the head, as if one is not surprised at all
A quick tensing of the body
A split second where breathing is suspended
Tightening the grip on whatever is being held
Shaking out the hands in an effort to relax once the initial shock has passed

> **WRITER'S TIP:** *With emotion, never be afraid to try something new. Individual expressions should be genuine but unique.*

SUSPICION

DEFINITION: suspecting, with little or no proof, that something is wrong

PHYSICAL SIGNALS:
Narrowing the eyes, squinting
Body angling away from suspect
A wrinkled brow
Flushed skin
A deliberate lowering of the head to study or stare
Arms tight to the body
Shooting glances at the suspect
Avoiding direct eye contact
A fake smile
Sneaking or spying
Eavesdropping
Following the suspected person
Keeping at a safe distance
Evaluating the subject's manner and appearance
Forced nonchalance to avoid the subject's notice (hands in pockets)
Crouching or leaning forward to get closer without being seen
Lips pressed flat
Recording the suspect's activity and movement (notes, pictures, etc.)
A set jaw
Head tilted while mentally weighing evidence
Being confrontational: *What are you doing here?* or *What do you want?*
Pointing a finger while confronting
Openly expressing distrust
Crossing the arms
Legs wide apart
A raised voice
Trying to convince others of the suspect's guilt
Big movements (waving arms while talking, counting out arguments on fingers)
Swaying from side to side
Arguing with the suspect
Pacing
Biting the inside of the lip
Sarcasm: *So you just happened to be near when my car's tires were slashed, huh?*
Questioning others as a way of gathering information
Googling the suspect

INTERNAL SENSATIONS:
Quickened breaths
Adrenaline rush
Thumping heartbeat

150

Fight-or-flight reflex kicking in
A knot in the belly
A sense of release when confronting the suspect

MENTAL RESPONSES:
Intent listening, so as to catch the suspect in their lie
Mentally running through everything known about the situation
Wanting to shield oneself and others from the person
Second guessing, fearing others will think one's concerns are irrational
Carefully preparing an argument or plan of attack
Weighing the danger level of the situation

CUES OF ACUTE OR LONG-TERM SUSPICION:
Obsession with the suspect
Stalking
Setting up the suspect in the hopes he will reveal his true self
Attempting to openly discredit or blackball the suspect
Contacting the appropriate authorities to express concern
Fantasizing about the day the suspect is finally exposed
MAY ESCALATE TO: FEAR (76), AGITATION (16), ANGER (22), PARANOIA (114)

CUES OF SUPPRESSED SUSPICION:
A slight head nod
Hmms, as opposed to overt agreement
A flat tone of voice
Noncommittal answers
Avoiding the suspected person
Agreeing too quickly, too loudly
Over-the-top support: *I'm with you 100%, I absolutely agree*
Nervous movements (biting nails, twisting a shirt button, rubbing the neck)
Standing back from the suspect, not stepping into his circle of friends
Spending minimum time with the suspect before finding a reason to leave

WRITER'S TIP: *While it's tempting to let a character speak openly about their emotions in dialogue, it will raise a red flag for the reader. If you wouldn't say it in real life, don't let your character.*

SYMPATHY

DEFINITION: sensitivity to and sharing in another's emotions

PHYSICAL SIGNALS:
Kind words, a soothing tone
Telling someone that they aren't alone, how things will work out
Rubbing someone's back
Squeezing a shoulder or hand
Lightly stroking a forearm
Offering a deep sigh and thoughtful expression
A parting hug lasting longer than normal
An understanding nod
Eyes narrowing, eyebrows pulling down in concentration
Crying with the person
Offering the bright side: *At least now we know*, or *It could have been worse*
Hugging, holding, pulling someone against your shoulder
Stroking or smoothing someone's hair
Clumsy attempts to comfort (a weak smile, an awkward hug)
Fumbling for words
Patting a leg in comfort
Leaning in, scooting closer
A gentle tone, using words the other person wants to hear
Phrasing questions in a positive way to make the other person feel better
Sitting with knees touching the other person's
Bringing a box of tissue or a cup of tea, unasked
Floundering hand movements
Pulling someone into a side hug
Handling distractions (answering the phone) so the other person won't have to
Apologizing, not out of accountability, but to voice the unfairness of the situation
Offering the advice of a relative or friend: *As my uncle used to say...*
Fussing over the person's appearance while speaking in encouraging tones
Listening intently while ignoring discomforts (cold, rain, heat)
Making sacrifices to offer comfort (cancelling plans)

*SPECIAL: Sympathetic physical signals between males
Saying *That sucks*, or *Yeah, I hear you*, or *I feel you, man*
A soft tap to the arm, a pat on the back
Lightly touching a shoulder
Listening, arms crossed over one's chest
Leaning in awkwardly with hands in the pockets, asking if things are okay
A heavy nod
Speaking in a quiet voice
A single shoulder shrug that breaks quickly
Listening while participating in another activity

Looking elsewhere while listening, so as not to make the other male uncomfortable
Offering to take him somewhere—a walk, a car ride, to hang out
Agreeing, even if he's being irrational
Letting him blow off steam or talk trash about others
Offering to avenge the offended party
Attempting to distract him (going to the movies, a party, drinking)

INTERNAL SENSATIONS:
Feeling emotionally drained
An overall weighted feeling
A slower heartbeat
Ache in the throat

MENTAL RESPONSES:
A desire to be near or to make physical contact
Wishing one could alleviate the pain
Uncertainty about what to say
Listening without judgment
Worry that this event could happen again, particularly to oneself or loved ones
Appreciation for the little things
The mind turning often to the person
Offering up prayers on their behalf
A narrowed focus, allowing for sole concentration on the other person
Relief

CUES OF ACUTE OR LONG-TERM SYMPATHY:
Obsessive thoughts on how to fix the situation
Employing clichés: *This too will pass, keep your chin up*, etc.
Giving comfort through gifts, plying a person with food or attention
Involving oneself in the situation, internalizing the other person's pain
MAY ESCALATE TO: SADNESS (134), ADORATION (14), LOVE (106), GRATITUDE (80), NOSTALGIA (110), WORRY (162)

CUES OF SUPPRESSED SYMPATHY:
A hand that lifts towards someone, then lowers
Speaking often of the person or situation
Privately praying for the person
Smiling or winking at the person but not offering verbal support
Watching at a distance, hoping for change

> **WRITER'S TIP:** *Emotions usually don't jump from mild to extreme in a short period of time. To gain the reader's trust, lay the proper foundation and show how stressors lead to a greater intensity.*

TERROR

DEFINITION: a state of extreme fear

PHYSICAL SIGNALS:
Rasping breaths
Bulging eyes, an inability to blink
Full body tremors
Bolting out of hiding, rushing away from the threat
Screaming, crying, blubbering
Speechlessness or incoherence
Holding oneself tightly (clutching the arms or wrapping arms around the belly)
Squeezing eyes shut
Moaning, whimpering
Trembling chin and lips
Running away with no destination in mind
Shaking one's head as if in denial
Clapping the hands over the ears
Pressing fists to the sides of the head
Crumpling, sinking to the ground
Retreating into the fetal position or curling up on the knees
Covering the face
Cringing, flinching, jumping at sounds
Tense muscles, rigid posture
A primal scream
Flaring nostrils
Grabbing onto another person, refusing to let go or leave them
Clumsiness (bumping into things, knocking things over)
Clutching the throat or chest
Gasping for air
Clammy skin
A harried, wild appearance
Clawing at the cheeks, dragging the fingers down
Tremors in the hands and fingers
Copious sweating
Risking a lesser danger in order to escape
Causing self-harm and not noticing (cuts, bruises, etc., while trying to escape)
Spinning around, trying to spot any and all danger
Backing away in quick, jerky steps from something or someone
Fight response (a rush attack, using anything at hand to hit or destroy)

INTERNAL SENSATIONS:
Hyperventilation
A racing pulse
Sound of heartbeat thrashing in the ears

A clenched jaw
High pain tolerance, not feeling or noticing injuries
Increased strength or stamina
Claustrophobia (even if one is not usually claustrophobic)
Pain in the chest, lungs, or throat
Weak legs
Increased sensitivity to every sound, touch, or change in the environment
Dizziness, seeing black spots

MENTAL RESPONSES:
A compulsion to look back (when fleeing)
Impaired decision making
A single-minded focus: to save oneself or someone else
Risk taking
Surrender if breaking point is reached
Hyper-vigilance
Thoughts that keep coming back to the worst possible outcome
Sensitivity to noise and movement

CUES OF ACUTE OR LONG-TERM TERROR:
Passing out from a stress overload, lack of oxygen, or both
A mental break (humming, rocking, hands over ears or eyes)
Heart attack
Shutting down mentally, retreating inward
Post Traumatic Stress Disorder
Insomnia
Hallucinations
Anxiety attacks
Weight loss
Nightmares
Depression
Substance abuse
Difficulties relating to others
Isolation
Phobias
MAY ESCALATE TO: PARANOIA (114), RAGE (120)

CUES OF SUPPRESSED TERROR:
Terror by nature is almost impossible to suppress or hide. Any attempt to hide
terror would simply display itself as FEAR (76)

WRITER'S TIP: *When conveying high emotion, keep the metaphors to a minimum. No matter how flowery or creative a character might be, in the midst of strong emotion, most people don't think in those terms. Keep it simple to maintain believability.*

UNCERTAINTY

DEFINITION: the state of being unsure; unable to commit to a course of action

PHYSICAL SIGNALS:
Biting the lip or inside of the cheek
Frowning
Glancing at others to see what they think
Looking down
Asking others for advice or opinions
Hands that fidget (twisting together, rubbing down the front of one's pants)
A downcast expression
Forehead wrinkling
Squinting, looking inward
Pinching or tugging on the bottom lip
Tilting the head from side to side, weighing choices
Rubbing the jaw or back of the neck
Pushing the hair out of the face
An impatient huff
Shuffling feet
Hesitating mid-action (while reaching for something or pulling out a wallet)
Starting a sentence with the word, *Well...*
Pulling back slightly
A grimace and a slight shake of the head
Asking questions to elicit more information
Making a *Hmmm* noise or throat clearing
Swallowing
Cracking the knuckles, or other 'stalling' gestures
Doodling on paper
Swaying or rocking on one's feet
Rubbing the lips or chin
Biting the inside of the cheek or bottom lip
Sighing
Rolling the neck
Tapping a pencil against a notepad or table
Jotting notes as a way to delay answering
Rounded shoulders, a slumped posture
Staring at nothing for an overlong moment
Talking through the options aloud
Asking for reassurance

INTERNAL SENSATIONS:
Breaths that catch in the chest
Tenseness in one's stomach
Increased thirst

MENTAL RESPONSES:
Feeling trapped
Indecision
Unease at one's options or choices
The mind racing through possibilities
Avoiding the person or issue
A desperate need to find answers
Feeling flustered by a less-than-ideal situation
Making decisions, then second-guessing oneself
Shutting down, refusing to make a decision

CUES OF ACUTE OR LONG-TERM UNCERTAINTY:
Self-doubt
Uncertainty that bleeds into other decisions and situations
Anger and frustration
Dismissing the situation without making a decision
Inability to make any decision on one's own
Researching (searching the web, speaking with professionals) to find answers
Going for a walk or leaving the situation in hopes of gaining a clear head
Repeatedly postponing or rescheduling events
An increased sense of desperation as time goes by and the situation is unresolved
MAY ESCALATE TO: CONFUSION (36), DENIAL (46), FRUSTRATION (78), UNEASE (158)

CUES OF SUPPRESSED UNCERTAINTY:
A delayed response
A noncommittal answer: *Maybe* or *We'll see*
Changing the topic to avoid hurt feelings or an argument
Diversion rather than open support
A hesitant nod
Stalling for time (pouring a glass of water and drinking)
Refusing to answer, letting the silence do the talking
Opening one's mouth to argue, then stopping
Acting noncommittal: *Let's put that in our back pocket for now, okay?*
Suggesting a vote of majority
Offering weak agreement or half-hearted support
Requesting more time to consider in order to delay
Passive-aggressiveness

WRITER'S TIP: *Maintain an overall perspective of emotional range as the story progresses from scene to scene. A strong manuscript will always expose the reader to contrasting emotional experiences that fit within the context of the POV character's growth.*

UNEASE

DEFINITION: a restlessness of the body or mind

PHYSICAL SIGNALS:
Shaking one's head
Crossing and uncrossing the arms or legs
Shifting in one's chair
Twisting or pulling at clothing
Slipping hands into pockets
Sidelong glances while keeping the head still
Tsking or making a noise in the throat
Leaning away from the source
Drawing back, making oneself smaller
Stopping to listen intently
A quick glance at the source, then away (a person, a clock, a door)
Chewing on a fingernail, picking at cuticles
Drawing the mouth into a straight line and biting the lip
Excessive swallowing
A shaky voice
Tugging clothes more firmly into place, closing an open jacket
Flipping hair or combing fingers through it
Hiding behind one's bangs
Being unnaturally quiet
Throat clearing
Frowning
Pushing food around on a plate
Gulping food down in order to escape more quickly
Trying to evade notice (slumping in a chair, withdrawing from conversation)
Turning slowly, unwillingly
Clutching an item tightly or holding it as a shield
Reluctantly speaking or approaching someone
Stilted, halting dialogue
A tapping heel
Checking a cell for messages or to see the time
Fiddling with jewelry or props
A swinging foot that suddenly goes still
Scrunching oneself up in a chair or sofa
Choosing a safe spot to wait
Flicking through a magazine without reading it
Lifting the chin in an attempt to look confident
Consciously forcing one's limbs to relax
Licking the lips
Tightening the hands into fists, then loosening them
Rigid posture

Nervous habits (picking off nail polish, humming under the breath)
Warm, sweaty hands
Constant motion (applying lip gloss, texting people, rooting in purse)

INTERNAL SENSATIONS:
A slight chill or shiver
Hair lifting on the back of the neck
A prickling of the scalp
A quiver in the stomach

MENTAL RESPONSES:
The feeling of being watched
Denial: *There's nothing wrong*, or *Stop overreacting.*
A feeling of being on edge
Impatience
Time feels like it's slowing down
Heightened watchfulness

CUES OF ACUTE OR LONG-TERM UNEASE:
Increased fidgeting, an inability to remain still
Pacing
An unshakeable sense of something being wrong
A need to leave, but not understanding why
Shifting from foot to foot
Feeling physically ill
Pretending to be unaware of a loud argument or uncomfortable situation
MAY ESCALATE TO: NERVOUSNESS (108), WORRY (162), FEAR (76)

CUES OF SUPPRESSED UNEASE:
Trying to slow one's breathing
Attempting to loosen up by rolling the shoulders
An unfocused gaze as one strives for mental calm
Walking away to gain composure
Wide eyes
A quick, false smile
Studiously not looking at the source
Keeping at a distance
Talking too fast

WRITER'S TIP: *To create a stronger reader reaction to emotion, remember to focus on showing what triggers the feeling, rather than only showing the character's response to it.*

WARINESS

DEFINITION: mistrust marked by caution and watchfulness; being alert to possible danger

PHYSICAL SIGNALS:
Head cocked to the side
Eyes narrowed, as if in confusion
Pursing the lips
Lowering the brows
Cutting the eyes toward the source
Hands up in a defensive stance
Speaking in a soothing, placating voice
Backing away
Posture "perks up" as awareness increases
Sidestepping, but keeping one's gaze on the source
Actively listening for something
Lifting the chin
Keeping one's hands free
Taking note of possible exits
Being aware of what lies behind
Asking questions to discern the root issue before things turn bad
Circling, approaching someone or something in a roundabout fashion
Slow, cautious movements
Speaking rapidly, with the intent of maintaining the status quo
Standing back and observing before jumping in
Stiffening and going still
A strained or tense voice
Flinching when touched
Hesitation
Lip biting or pressing the lips together
A probing gaze
Careful words
A furrowed brow
Rubbing at the forehead or temples
Gritting the teeth
A stern or serious expression
A jutting jaw
Alert to sudden movements

INTERNAL SENSATIONS:
Increased adrenaline
Rapid heartbeat and pulse
Tense muscles
Breath that catches or stops briefly

An intuitive feeling that something isn't right (hairs standing up, prickling of skin)

MENTAL RESPONSES:
Mind tries to discern possible danger
Trusting one's gut feelings
Heightened senses
Defensiveness
Racing thoughts while trying to make sense of the situation
Confusion
Difficulty committing fully to any action
A finely-tuned sense of observation
Trying to see and hear everything at once
An inability to relax or smile
Thinking ahead to what might happen

CUES OF ACUTE OR LONG-TERM WARINESS:
Increasing one's personal space
Positioning oneself to create a barrier (moving behind a table, etc.)
Arguing without aggression, only to provide insight
Scanning for potential weapons
Asking questions one knows the answers to in an effort to discern another's intent
MAY ESCALATE TO: ANXIETY (30), FEAR (76), UNEASE (158), SUSPICION (150)

CUES OF SUPPRESSED WARINESS:
Standoffishness
Looking from lowered lids
Attempting to lighten the mood with a joke
A posture that suggests discomfort (standing by oneself, clamping the hands around the waist)
Leaning away
Hesitation

> **WRITER'S TIP:** *When writing emotion, pull from your own past. Even if you haven't experienced what the POV character is going through, chances are you've felt the same emotion about something else. Draw on your personal experience and bring life to the story.*

WORRY

DEFINITION: mental distress that arises from disturbing thoughts, usually regarding some anticipated event

PHYSICAL SIGNALS:
Wrinkling the brow
Biting one's lip
Pinching the skin at the throat
Feet that bounce or tap
Pulling or twisting at one's hair
Pacing
Drinking too much coffee, smoking too much
Circles under the eyes
Eyebrows drawing together
Tossing and turning in bed, an inability to sleep
Asking too many questions
Stroking or rubbing an eyebrow
Rumpled, unwashed clothes
Rubbing one's hands on pant legs
Lank or unwashed hair
Poor communication with others
Repeatedly rubbing the face
A gaze that flits around the room, never settling on a person or object for long
Clinging to loved ones
Taking deep breaths in an effort to calm oneself
Pointless activity as a way to stay busy
Calling in sick
Stooped posture
Clutching at a sweater, purse, or necklace for comfort
Biting the nails, chewing on a knuckle
Running a jerky hand through the hair
Smoothing and re-smoothing clothing
Clasping one's hands together
A stiff neck, strained muscles
A pained or watery gaze
Throat clearing
Blinking less (as if worried one might miss something)
Fidgeting, having a hard time sitting still
Sitting, then standing, then sitting again

INTERNAL SENSATIONS:
A loss of appetite
A sensitive stomach
Heartburn or other digestive issues

Dry mouth
Constricted throat

MENTAL RESPONSES:
Uncertainty over choices made
An unwillingness to leave a certain place (phone, house, car)
An inability to focus
A need to control
Regret for a past action
Distancing oneself from others
Reading into things, over-analyzing
Assuming the worst-case scenario
Over-protectiveness
Irritability

CUES OF ACUTE OR LONG-TERM WORRY:
Weight loss
Premature gray
New wrinkles
Slipping grades at school, poor performance at work
Ulcers
Anxiety attacks
Panic disorders
High blood pressure
Heart disease
Increased sickness due to compromised immune system
Insomnia and fatigue
Hypochondria
MAY ESCALATE TO: WARINESS (160), FEAR (76), ANXIETY (30),
PARANOIA (114), DREAD (64)

CUES OF SUPPRESSED WORRY:
Furtively watching the clock or door
Jumpiness
A strained or faked smile
Adopting new hobbies to distract oneself
Putting up a false front as if everything is okay
A shortened attention span
Humming that feels forced, or fades quickly after it starts
Going about one's daily activities with the mind somewhere else

WRITER'S TIP: *Weather details can add texture and meaning to a scene. Consider how a character's mood can shift because of the weather. It can also stand in the way of their goals, providing tension.*

RECOMMENDED READING

The Definitive Book of Body Language (Allan & Barbara Pease)

Characters, Emotion & Viewpoint (Nancy Kress)

Creating Character Emotion (Ann Hood)

Telling Lies: Clues to Deceit in the Marketplace, Politics, and Marriage (Paul Ekman)

Dear Reader,

If you found *The Emotion Thesaurus* a useful companion to your creative process, we'd love to hear about your experience. Honest reviews on Goodreads, Amazon and Barnes & Noble are always appreciated. And if you would like to explore some of the other Descriptive Thesaurus Collections we have created for writers, please visit us at WritersHelpingWriters.net.

To help you create compelling characters with realistic strengths, weaknesses, motivations, and emotional wounds, please check out our other books, *The Positive Trait Thesaurus: A Writer's Guide to Character Attributes* and *The Negative Trait Thesaurus: A Writer's Guide to Character Flaws.*

Happy writing!

Angela & Becca